# Mindful
## Assessment

*The 6 Essential Fluencies of Innovative Learning*

Lee Watanabe Crockett
Andrew Churches

Solution Tree | Press

*a division of*
Solution Tree

555 North Morton Street
Bloomington, IN 47404
800.733.6786 (toll free) / 812.336.7700
FAX: 812.336.7790

email: info@SolutionTree.com
SolutionTree.com

Visit **go.SolutionTree.com/assessment** to download the free reproducibles in this book.

Printed in the United States of America

20   19   18   17   16                    1   2   3   4   5

Library of Congress Cataloging-in-Publication Data

Names: Crockett, Lee, author. | Churches, Andrew, author.

Title: Mindful assessment : the 6 essential fluencies of innovative learning

/ Lee Watanabe Crockett and Andrew Churches.

Description: Bloomington, IN : Solution Tree Press, [2017] | Includes

bibliographical references and index.

Identifiers: LCCN 2016028649 | ISBN 9781942496885 (perfect bound)

Subjects: LCSH: Educational tests and measurements--United States. | Academic

achievement--United States--Testing. | Education--United

States--Evaluation.

Classification: LCC LB3051 .C73 2017 | DDC 371.260973--dc23 LC record available at https://lccn.loc.gov/2016028649

**Solution Tree**
Jeffrey C. Jones, CEO
Edmund M. Ackerman, President

**Solution Tree Press**
*President:* Douglas M. Rife
*Editorial Director:* Tonya Maddox Cupp
*Managing Production Editor:* Caroline Weiss
*Senior Production Editor:* Tara Perkins
*Senior Editor:* Amy Rubenstein
*Copy Chief:* Sarah Payne-Mills
*Copy Editors:* Miranda Addonizio and Ashante K. Thomas
*Proofreader:* Elisabeth Abrams
*Text Designer:* Abigail Bowen
*Cover Designer:* Rian Anderson
*Editorial Assistant:* Jessi Finn
*Editorial Intern:* Laura Dzubay

We dedicate this book to all those involved in the education of our youth. It is you who inspire our future artists, innovators, scientists, and leaders. Although children are only a small percentage of the population, they are 100 percent of the future. We thank you for your selfless commitment to our children and to creating a bright future for all.

# Acknowledgments

We would like to thank the small army of help we always have behind us. Thanks to Mia, Tania, Jordan, Ross, Heather, Alex, Lisa, Simon, and all the rest of the Global Digital Citizen Foundation Ninjas. We also thank the teachers and schools that have embraced this work and become true champions, especially Jane, Heather, Belinda, Peter, Joan, Jackie, and Simon.

Solution Tree Press would like to thank the following reviewers:

Bo Adams
Chief Learning and Innovation Officer
Mount Vernon Presbyterian School
Atlanta, Georgia

Rose Arnell
K–12 Gifted Teacher and
    Technology Specialist
Nagel Middle School
Cincinnati, Ohio

W. Blake Busbin
Advanced Placement U.S.
    History Teacher
Auburn High School
Auburn, Alabama

Stephanie Carbonneau
French Teacher
York Middle School
York, Maine

Robert DoBell
Superintendent
Three Forks School District
Three Forks, Montana

Dolores Gende
Instructional Technology and Honors
    Physics Teacher
Parish Episcopal School
Dallas, Texas

Kevin Grawer
Principal
Maplewood Richmond Heights
  High School
St. Louis, Missouri

Allison Hogan
Primer Teacher
The Episcopal School of Dallas
Dallas, Texas

Jen Laubscher
Project-Based Learning Teacher Trainer
  and Coach
Onondaga-Cortland-Madison Board of
  Cooperative Educational Services
Syracuse, New York

Olivia Lozano
First and Second Grade Teacher
University of California, Los Angeles
  Lab School
Los Angeles, California

Julie E. McDaniel
Educational Consultant
Oakland Schools
Waterford, Michigan

Bonnie Nieves
Science Teacher
Millbury Memorial Junior/Senior
  High School
Millbury, Massachusetts

Bill Powers
Principal
Cherokee Middle School
Springfield Public Schools
Springfield, Missouri

David Wees
Assessment Specialist
New Visions
New York, New York

Lisa Zeller
Seventh Grade Science Teacher
World of Inquiry School No. 58
Rochester, New York

Visit **go.SolutionTree.com/assessment** to download
the free reproducibles in this book.

# Table of Contents

About the Authors .............................................................................. xiii

Preface ............................................................................................ xv

## *Introduction*

Lessons From the Dojo ......................................................................... 1

    Assessment Best Practices .............................................................. 2

    Changing Methods for a Changing World ........................................ 4

    Big Picture Schools and the Future of Assessment ........................... 5

    Structure of This Book .................................................................. 7

## *Chapter 1*

Approaches to Assessment .................................................................... 9

    The Learning Process .................................................................. 10

    Diagnostic Assessment ............................................................... 12

        Deliberate and Purposeful Assessment ................................... 14

        Forms of Diagnostic Assessment ............................................ 15

    Formative Assessment ................................................................ 18

    High-Quality Feedback ................................................................ 20

    Guiding Questions ..................................................................... 24

## *Chapter 2*

## Structure of the Fluencies Assessment Framework.............. 25

Phases of the Assessment Framework................................................26

Criterion-Based Assessment Tools....................................................28

Common Language of Assessment ........................................................29

Evidence Statements.................................................................................31

Exemplars of Student Work....................................................................32

Modifications for Measurement.............................................................34

Guiding Questions ...............................................................................36

## *Chapter 3*

## Solution Fluency............................................................................ 37

Define..................................................................................................37

Discover ..............................................................................................38

Dream..................................................................................................39

Design.................................................................................................40

Deliver.................................................................................................42

Debrief.................................................................................................43

Solution Fluency in Schools...............................................................44

Brainy Inventions (Primary School)........................................................45

Hidden Treasure (Primary School).........................................................45

Photo Power (Middle School) .................................................................45

Design Star (Middle School)...................................................................45

Off to Space (High School).....................................................................46

Feeding the Need (High School).............................................................46

Rubrics for Solution Fluency .............................................................46

Guiding Questions ..............................................................................54

## *Chapter 4*

## Information Fluency ....................................................................... 57

Ask......................................................................................................57

Acquire ...............................................................................................59

Analyze ................................................................................................................60

Apply ..................................................................................................................63

Assess ................................................................................................................64

Information Fluency in Schools .........................................................................65

    Idol History (Primary School) ......................................................................65

    Gratitude Group (Primary School) ..............................................................65

    Lead the Way (Middle School) ...................................................................66

    Party Planners (Middle School) ..................................................................66

    Green Gears (High School) .........................................................................66

    The Future Is Now (High School) ................................................................67

Rubrics for Information Fluency ........................................................................67

Guiding Questions .............................................................................................73

## Chapter 5

Creativity Fluency ..............................................................................................75

Identify ...............................................................................................................75

Inspire ................................................................................................................77

Interpolate .........................................................................................................78

Imagine ..............................................................................................................79

Inspect ...............................................................................................................79

Creativity Fluency in Schools ...........................................................................80

    Magic Mystery (Primary School) ................................................................81

    The Light Painters (Primary School) ..........................................................81

    FUNderwater (Middle School) ...................................................................81

    Design Star (Middle School) ......................................................................82

    Mock Doc (High School) ............................................................................82

    Break the Silence (High School) .................................................................82

Rubrics for Creativity Fluency ...........................................................................83

Guiding Questions .............................................................................................87

## Chapter 6

Media Fluency .....................................................................................................89

Listen ..................................................................................................................89

Message ...................................................................................................... 90

Medium ..................................................................................................... 90

Leverage ........................................................................................................ 91

Message ...................................................................................................... 91

Medium ...................................................................................................... 92

Media Fluency in Schools ..................................................................................... 93

Mathematics Models (Primary School) ............................................................. 93

Faraway Friends (Primary School) ................................................................... 94

Looking Back (Middle School) ........................................................................ 94

Game Builders (Middle School) ...................................................................... 94

Mock Doc (High School) ................................................................................ 95

Selling an Idea (High School) ......................................................................... 95

Rubrics for Media Fluency ..................................................................................... 95

Guiding Questions .............................................................................................. 102

## Chapter 7

## Collaboration Fluency .......................................................................................... 103

Establish ........................................................................................................ 103

Envision ......................................................................................................... 105

Engineer ......................................................................................................... 106

Execute ........................................................................................................... 106

Examine .......................................................................................................... 107

Collaboration Fluency in Schools ........................................................................ 108

Citizenship Day (Primary School) ................................................................... 108

Tour Guide (Primary School) ......................................................................... 109

Atomic Rock (Middle School) ........................................................................ 109

Party Planners (Middle School) ...................................................................... 110

The Greenway (High School) ......................................................................... 110

Irrational Land (High School) ......................................................................... 110

Rubrics for Collaboration Fluency ........................................................................ 111

Guiding Questions .............................................................................................. 117

*Chapter 8*

## Global Digital Citizenship

Global Digital Citizenship ..................................................................119

Personal Responsibility ................................................................. 119

Global Citizenship ........................................................................121

Digital Citizenship .......................................................................121

Altruistic Service.........................................................................123

Environmental Stewardship .........................................................124

Global Digital Citizenship in Schools .............................................125

Schooled on the Future (Primary School).........................................125

Citizenship Day (Primary School) .................................................125

Gratitude Group (Primary School)................................................126

Welcome, World! (Middle School)................................................126

Radical Recyclers (Middle School) ...............................................126

Get What You Give (High School) ................................................127

Biodiversity Database (High School) .............................................127

Rubrics for Global Digital Citizenship ............................................128

Guiding Questions ......................................................................138

*Epilogue*

Where Will You Go From Here?.....................................................141

*Appendix*

Glossary of Command Terms .......................................................143

References and Resources ..................................................................145

Index...............................................................................................151

# About the Authors

**Lee Watanabe Crockett** is an optimist. He believes in a bright future and our ability to build it together through connection and compassion. He is an author, speaker, designer, inspirational thinker, and the creative force behind some of the most exciting transformations in education happening worldwide. In life, Lee believes in creating balance in the reality of a digital present and future. As such, he has cultivated skills in aikido, studied the traditional tea ceremony while living in Japan, and studied painting in Italy. He also studies traditional Zen Buddhist music, which he performs on a *shakuhachi*, a Japanese bamboo flute.

Lee is curious about life and the shared human experience. This curiosity is infectious, as anyone who has heard Lee speak can tell you. Joyful curiosity is the foundation of his approach to creating vital learning and corporate environments for groups around the world.

Lee is coauthor of *Understanding the Digital Generation*, *The Digital Diet*, *Living on the Future Edge*, and the bestseller *Literacy Is Not Enough*. He works with educators and corporations in several countries, helping them make the shift to regain relevance and establish a culture of excellence.

To learn more about Lee's work, visit http://globaldigitalcitizen.org or www .leewatanabecrockett.com, or follow @leecrockett on Twitter.

 **Andrew Churches** is a teacher and information and communication technology enthusiast. He teaches at Kristin School, a school with a mobile computing program that teaches students with personal mobile devices and laptops, on the North Shore of Auckland, New Zealand. He is the coauthor of *The Digital Diet* and *Apps for Learning*.

Andrew is also an edublogger, wiki author, and innovator. In 2008, Andrew's wiki, Educational Origami, was nominated for the Edublog Awards' Best Educational Wiki award. He contributes to a number of websites and blogs, including *Tech & Learning* magazine, *Spectrum Education* magazine, and *The Committed Sardine Blog*. Andrew believes that to prepare our students for the future, we must prepare them for change and teach them to question, think, adapt, and modify.

To learn more about Andrew's work, visit http://globaldigitalcitizen.org, or follow @achurches on Twitter.

To book Lee Watanabe Crockett or Andrew Churches for professional development, contact pd@SolutionTree.com.

# Preface

Every year, we give hundreds of presentations around the globe, and we have talked with tens of thousands of educators about what skills they feel students will require to be successful in the 21st century. Lee met with representatives of a major multinational company in Australia that is heavily involved in the mining and smelter industries. He asked what skills they measure when considering new employees and if these criteria have changed over time. In the past, the physical capability of a potential employee was one of their major considerations, along with how well he or she could follow instructions. Now the two main attributes they seek are completely different: real-time problem solving and collaboration. Companies have invested significant amounts of money in systems and training to try to develop these attributes in their employees but have found it so expensive and so difficult that they instead have shifted to investing in hiring practices that maximize the prospect of hiring employees who already strongly possess these skills. They give these new hiring criteria more weight than education or experience.

As factories automated or relocated to Asia during the first wave of outsourcing, entire Western cities seemingly disappeared (Janz, 2011). Not only have populations decreased drastically in many manufacturing cities, but for those who remain, economic hardship and its real-life consequences persist (Applebaum, 2015; Padnani, 2013). While the first wave was a physical relocation to another part of the world, the second great wave is relocation to the virtual world, and it is well underway. As a result of this shift to a global economy, millions of people have gone from working for one company for many years to a continual churn of many companies at one time (Friedman, 2005; Lee & Mather, 2008; Marker, 2015; Pink, 2011). For many, this has caused a shift from an employee mindset to an entrepreneurial mindset, and the skills required to succeed are very different for each. Outside the world of academia, employers place little importance on what people know; what matters is what they can do with what they know—their skills.

In our book *Literacy Is Not Enough* (Crockett, Jukes, & Churches, 2011), we identify a list of essential skills our students will need to become the successful architects of a future world that we can only imagine and the masters of challenges we can't imagine.

Learners must have:

- The ability to *solve problems* in real time as well as a system and strategy for solving more complex problems over extended time periods

- The skills to *think and work creatively* in digital and nondigital environments to develop unique and useful solutions by both adapting and improving on current designs as well as the innovation of new possibilities

- The ability to *think analytically* using skills such as comparing, contrasting, evaluating, synthesizing, and applying without instruction or supervision (the higher-order thinking skills of Bloom's taxonomy)

- The ability to *interact and work seamlessly* in both face-to-face and online environments with real and virtual partners, capitalizing on the unique perspectives and opportunities presented in a collective of differing ages, gender, cultural backgrounds, nationalities, and physical locations

- The skills to *communicate in multiple multimedia formats*, such as with video and imagery, as actively as they would when communicating through text or speech, determining both the message's content and desired outcome and selecting the most appropriate medium for the message and audience, as well as the skills to analyze communication by separating the message from the media and evaluating the efficacy and authenticity of both

- The qualities of *ethics*, *action*, and *accountability* through personal responsibility, environmental awareness, altruistic service, and global and digital citizenship, as well as the ability to evaluate oneself and one's colleagues, considering the attributes of accountability, integrity, compassion, curiosity, courage, independence, balance, perseverance, resilience, and reflection

These skills are based on a broader set of fluencies, which we identify in *Literacy Is Not Enough* as the *21st century fluencies*. We will henceforth refer to these as the *essential fluencies*. These include the following.

- **Solution fluency:** The ability to clearly define the problem, design an appropriate solution, deliver the solution, and evaluate the process and the outcome to creatively solve problems in real time is solution fluency. The 6Ds—(1) define, (2) discover, (3) dream, (4) design, (5) deliver, and (6) debrief—define solution fluency.

- **Information fluency:** The ability to unconsciously and intuitively interpret information in all forms and formats in order to extract essential knowledge, perceive its meaning and significance, and utilize it to complete real-world tasks is information fluency. The 5As—(1) ask, (2) acquire, (3) analyze, (4) apply, and (5) assess—define this process.

- **Creativity fluency:** Artistic proficiency adds meaning through design, art, and storytelling in this process. It is about using innovative design to add value to the function of a product through its form. The 5Is—(1) identify, (2) inspire, (3) interpolate, (4) imagine, and (5) inspect—define the creativity fluency process.

- **Media fluency:** The ability to look critically at any medium, effectively evaluating both the medium and the message, and also to select and produce the most appropriate and effective media for communicating an intended message is media fluency. There are 2Ls to media fluency—(1) listening and (2) leveraging. These apply to both the intended message and the medium used for delivering the message.

- **Collaboration fluency:** This refers to teams whose working proficiency is such that they have reached the unconscious ability to work cooperatively with virtual and real partners in online environments to create original digital products. The 5Es—(1) establish, (2) envision, (3) engineer, (4) execute, and (5) examine—define the collaboration fluency process.

- **Global digital citizenship:** Students learn the fluencies within the context of being a global digital citizen. This citizen is a conscientious, respectful, and compassionate individual who strives to establish a sense of global community in all online and offline relationships and endeavors. The five unique tenets—(1) personal responsibility, (2) global citizenship, (3) digital citizenship, (4) altruistic service, and (5) environmental stewardship—define global digital citizenship.

These are the crucial new skills and mindsets that learners need to flourish in 21st century life. But what do we mean when we say *fluency*, and why is it important? Let's start by taking a brief look at the etymology of the word itself. Fluent comes from the Latin *fluentem*, which means to be relaxed and flowing. Consider the following comparison that perfectly describes how this concept applies to the ideal nature of 21st century skills.

Do you think about the action of using a ballpoint pen to write something down? Is it a process in which you must concentrate and focus on holding the pen, making the strokes, and dotting and crossing the letters appropriately? Of course not—you pick up the pen and you write. It's not a conscious consideration or a step-by-step operation you give your attention to. You just write. So you could refer to this ability as *pen fluency* or *handwriting fluency* because you know it so well that you don't think about it when you do it.

We should foster the essential fluencies in our students in exactly the same way. The fluencies comprise specific stages, all of which students can learn, use, and improve until they're second nature. We must aspire to help our students reach this level of familiarity and automatic command when developing 21st century skills to prepare them for productive and prosperous lives.

Though the language may vary, our conversations with stakeholders (from parents to national-level officials) all over the world reflect a widely shared vision that involves students acquiring these skills. These are the true long-term educational goals we need to achieve. The questions are: Are our students developing these critical skills in the mandated curriculum, and is there a system in place for us to evaluate and ensure that students properly develop them?

# Lessons From the Dojo

To some who have watched aikido in a movie or YouTube clip, it appears that one person is simply tossing around another. It seems almost impossible that such tiny movements could cause such a major reaction, and that perhaps there is a little overreacting involved. To others, the actions seem to be magical, almost superhuman, as if the practitioners call on unseen forces to execute the movements so fluidly and with such precision.

In aikido practice, the *uke*, or receiver, initiates the move by attacking the *shite*, or doer, who applies the *waza*, or technique, to the receiver. Both sides, the doing and receiving, of the technique must be learned and are essential to a balanced practice of the art. The shite moves the body to blend with the uke's actions. The uke then must blend with the shite's technique in a way that is not a mere passive reception of, but rather a thoroughly active response to, the shite's actions. While the uke appears to make exaggerated movements of falling and rolling, these actions are the only way one can safely receive the technique. To be passive in the process exposes the uke to serious injury. It is a process of harmony and unification, not of physical strength.

One December morning, Lee was training with another student at an aikido dojo in Kyoto, Japan. During their practice, Lee became distracted, but his daydreaming was quickly interrupted by a searing pain in his shoulder and the sting of his face slamming into the frozen bamboo-weave tatami mats.

As Lee snapped back to reality and grasped his shoulder, he saw his shite was also lying on the tatami and holding his shoulder. The realization of what had just happened came rushing back. In receiving the waza and not being present, he had strongly resisted the shite who was also not in the moment. Both Lee and his partner received injuries that prevented them from training for a week but were not serious enough to prevent them, at the insistence of their sensei, from cleaning the dojo with their uninjured arms, each with one hand on the rag at all times, cleaning, wringing, and cleaning more, to remind them of the importance of working together in harmony, to the benefit of all—a basic aikido tenet, a term which means *the way of unifying heart and spirit.*

Before resuming training, the sensei reminded Lee of a valuable perspective on mindfully training in the art of aikido: To study aikido, we must be mindful at all times. Not for our own protection, but because we are responsible for others. If you are tired, or cannot be present, you must respectfully withdraw for everyone's benefit. This, too, is to take responsibility for others. The shite must be mindful in the speed and intensity of the waza, constantly adjusting to use his or her capability. But the uke has even greater responsibility to be even more mindful of the shite's ability and waza and provide measured and appropriate resistance and submission. Only this way can the shite improve the waza. Each party must be mindful and care for the other so all can grow.

Often we refer to teaching and learning as though they consist of simply applying teaching to learners, with learning happening as a direct result. However, just as the shite does not do the technique to the uke but rather unifies with the uke in the process, we must unify with our students. Our thinking about what it means to teach must be framed as a response to learning, with assessment as the method through which the learner understands how to improve. We should not see learning as the outcome of teaching but rather allow teaching to become a mindful response to learning.

Teachers do not create learning; only learners create learning. Teachers should respond to student performance to guide the learning process. This happens through mindful assessment, being conscious and in the moment, seeing the situation clearly, and using assessment to confirm or create this clarity. In short, what we are advocating for is a formative approach to feedback rather than the summative approach that is so pervasive in the standardized testing culture in our schools.

## Assessment Best Practices

In practicing aikido, the sensei would never simply tell a student, "That was 74 percent." Instead, the sensei would watch mindfully and comment on what needs improvement, demonstrate it, and then provide the opportunity to improve. Similarly, a parent teaching a child to cook would never say, "That was 74 percent." Instead, like the sensei, the parent would watch, demonstrate, and allow the child a chance to get better. These acts of mindful nurturing and guidance are examples of natural learning, and we perform them instinctively. It makes complete sense to us and is implemented in every context except in school.

A number or percentage means little and accomplishes even less. This type of summative feedback in the classroom only serves to give the student a sense of finality, as if to say, "This number is the best measure of your capabilities—this is all you've got in you." A percentage does not define the specific areas in which the student needs to improve, and it fails to acknowledge what the student has done well, providing little constructive feedback or meaning.

Most assessment that occurs in schools, though, is summative. This is how success (or failure) in the school system is judged—the school judges whether the student is ready for the next grade, universities judge whether the student is eligible for admission, and governments and citizens judge the school and even the teacher. Learning is measured in a final examination or series of examinations that culminates in an educational experience for the year, term, semester, and so on. These summative exams are, in fact, many schools' primary assessment. If it has marks or grades that cannot be altered through further learning, it is summative—regardless of when it appears in the term. Summative assessment is what parents are familiar with, it is what politicians know, and it is what employers understand (Churches, n.d.). It is a summation of how "effective" and "successful" students are during a specific period in time. It is for this reason that there has been intense focus on standardized summative assessment in many countries.

Educators use summative assessment to provide brief reflections of educational success (or failure). It shows them, as well as administrators, district and departmental leaders, and government officers, how the school, students, and administration progress. According to Churches (n.d.):

> There is nothing wrong with this type of assessment as long as we take it in the context of a snapshot—a brief moment frozen in time. It is, however, a poor reflection of a student's total learning experience. How can you condense a student's learning career into one three-hour examination? (p. 7)

How can we reduce the human experience to a number? Is it really possible for this approach to clearly and accurately determine how well a student truly learns, absorbs, and uses knowledge? And yet, this is a traditional, standard approach to assessment that schools employ globally. Policymakers consider it in many cases the proof and rationale they need to take severe actions on major issues, including performance-based pay, job retention, and school funding.

And while this educational model holds the schools, the administration, and the teachers accountable for the learning, the only group that it doesn't hold accountable is the students. Summative assessment provides no opportunity or responsibility for the learner improvement. It is a judgment, and it is final.

The challenge we face is that the summative approach to pedagogy and assessment does not fit into the reality of curricular reforms such as the National Governors Association Center for Best Practices and Council of Chief State School Officers' Common Core State Standards for English language arts and mathematics (NGA & CCSSO, 2010a, 2010b) that focus on developing skills rather than memorizing facts. Transitioning to the Common Core and skills-based teaching approaches requires a complete transformation of both pedagogical and assessment practices.

# Changing Methods for a Changing World

We live in a world of 24/7 content and a sea of online information. This has transformed our students from consumers of content into what we call *prosumers*—simultaneous content producers and consumers. "They expect and demand transparency, adaptability, contextual and collaborative learning, and the opportunity to use technology. These changes shape the pedagogy we need to employ to engage and motivate our learners" (Churches, n.d., p. 7). Students are living in a world where the only constant is change. It is a world of adaptation, continuous adjustments, and incremental improvements. It follows that the ways we teach and assess students should mirror this reality.

We see these practices clearly in lean methodology, which has its roots in software design but has become a global business movement. In the old software-development world, a company would take months if not years to develop a product, which it would then box, stock, market, and hopefully sell—all at great expense of the precious resources of personnel, time, and money. The risk in this model is enormous. If the researchers, marketers, or anyone in the supply chain gets it wrong, it can lead to company failure.

The lean methodology is a complete revolution in thinking about product development and how to best meet a customer base's needs. A lean startup company builds what is referred to as the *minimum viable product* (MVP)—the most efficient and simplest version of how to meet an existing need. It places all extra features and ideas for expansion in a development queue, and then it launches the product. The users' power takes over at this stage. How do they use the product? What do they like and dislike about it? What do they want to do with it that they cannot do right now? The development team works to change the product in "sprints" of activity. The company brings forward ideas generated by the users or from the development queue, then designs, programs, and implements them. However, this is not to say that they will be permanent. The company evaluates every change, and the company pulls the feature if the users don't like it or don't use it. In the old software development world, this would not, and could not, be the case. Since considerable effort and expense went into its development, a company would just leave it in place. This may make the developer feel better, but the poor user ends up with bloatware—unwanted software that makes the system run slowly. Versions of Microsoft Word, for example, have had more than twelve hundred functions in all the various menus and submenus, which might be more than any user would ever care to explore.

This new approach to business exemplifies monumental incremental change—changing everything by constantly changing small things. It's a constant cycle of creating new product, measuring impact, adjusting the activities, evaluating the options, and creating a new product again based on the new knowledge. It also means that a company can turn on a dime, or *pivot* as it's referred to in lean methodology, in response to the users. Lean startups use constant formative feedback to continuously learn and improve—there is no end point, and the learning and improving can go on indefinitely. This model of lean methodology involves a type of mindfulness, as developers are continually aware of where they currently are and where they need to go, reflecting on their product and making adjustments. This highly efficient process illustrates the type of formative assessment we are advocating for in classrooms. When teachers are mindful of a student's state, they can identify what learning needs to shift throughout the process in order to improve rather than assigning a summative value to the student's learning after it has completed. Just as with the old software-development method, such summative assessment runs the risk of realizing that key factors are missing after it is too late to address them.

For the 21st century learner, or for any learner, summative assessment is not ideal. Formative assessment fits much better with student needs, and also with the teaching and learning outcomes schools have in place. Happily, there is a wonderful transformation happening inside education to make the shift to the same mindful assessment that is already present in all other natural learning experiences in our lives.

# Big Picture Schools and the Future of Assessment

One argument for preserving standardized testing at the secondary level is that universities use these results for admissions, making it seem as if it is the only option for students who are university hopefuls. However, the reality is that, because we know that standardized testing inadequately measures unique and differentiated learners, we are starting to see some change. Increasing competition for students among postsecondary institutions has started a radical shift in entrance criteria.

We have been working with Australian schools affiliated with the nonprofit Big Picture Education Australia (www.bigpicture.org.au), which allows students different ways to work toward the same standards required in traditional schooling and is focused on cultivating exceptional learners. They offer a parallel path to the same curricular outcomes. In Big Picture schools, learning is largely self-determined and self-directed. Students choose areas that personally interest them for intensive inquiry, yet still must demonstrate their understanding of the curriculum. How they learn it, insofar as the context, is largely up to them, but again, they are aware of the required standards and that they are responsible for determining how to demonstrate them. In our experience, students are highly engaged in the process. They usually build their own assessments, which faculty moderate. So from the very start, they have an awareness and understanding of the curriculum and the success criteria required to demonstrate their learning, and have built an assessment as an end point. All this happens before the learning begins. In our observation, this is actually a very deep learning process from the start. We believe that students identifying success criteria and developing their own assessments build their capacity to be life-long independent learners and enjoy successful lives.

Many students in Big Picture schools are exceptionally talented young people who do not fit well in the traditional school system. *Big picture* sounds very broad, but in fact creates an environment where teachers can really cultivate talent and nurture potential in individual students with amazing results. Throughout the program at Melrose High School in Pearce, Australia, for example, learners explore their interests through excursions within and outside their community, in-depth projects, and internships. It includes students from both year 11 and year 12. According to Big Picture Education Australia (2011), year 12 requirements include the following.

- Demonstrate heightened personal qualities and depth of work.
- Play a leadership role in the school.
- Mentor a younger student.
- Complete an in-depth senior thesis project.
- Write a seventy-five- to one-hundred-page autobiography.
- Complete a post-school portfolio, which is a cumulative product of not only learning outcomes but evidence of the learning process.
- Visit and interview with at least four universities or TAFE (Technical and Further Education) colleges, which are similar to technology or vocational post-secondary institutes in North America.
- Research and apply to a university or TAFE college.
- Update a personal exhibition developed throughout the years for post-school use (resume, transcripts, essay, awards, best work).
- Create a post–high school plan.
- Present work and reflections at a graduation exhibition.

These are substantial requirements, and Australian universities are taking notice. Moving beyond standardized testing has not only provided these universities with a better picture of potential students but also genuinely improved the participating students' education experience. Several Australian universities have now begun working on a formal process and are now accepting Big Picture students based on a portfolio of their work rather than a traditional year 12 certification (similar to the U.S. high school diploma).

With a shift to that mindful state of nurturing the student, we in turn nurture ourselves, regain relevance, and establish a culture of excellence. We intend for this book to support those educators and educational institutions that are embracing a bright future for education through inquiry- and project-based, student-centered learning. It is a guide to assessing the essential skills of problem solving, collaboration, creativity, and analytical thinking for success in the world today or for anyone wanting to engage in authentic, transparent, mindful assessment.

## Structure of This Book

In this book, we first discuss various assessment methods and make the case for using formative assessment as the best way to gain insight into student understanding and simultaneously improve that understanding. Chapter 1 examines phases of learning and their alignment with assessment methods and skill acquisition. Chapter 2 explains the structure of the framework we have devised for assessing the essential fluencies outlined in the preface. It offers tools and processes for developing assessments to appraise the skills, tasks, and products involved in students' acquisition of the fluencies in the classroom. Chapters 3 through 8 each examine one fluency in depth, noting the numerous unique aspects that contribute to each fluency and outlining the skills and processes these aspects develop in students and how they are beneficial. We describe possible classroom lessons and projects that teachers may apply and provide guiding questions within each fluency. Then, we provide a detailed assessment rubric to assist teachers in identifying students' abilities within the fluencies and allowing them to set goals for student growth in these areas. A glossary of command terms rounds out the book.

# chapter

## 1

# Approaches to Assessment

What is the most common feedback we provide to students? A number. It is intended to be helpful, to provide a snapshot of where they are in their learning. Even if it doesn't affect the overall grade, even if it is just a quiz, we provide a number. The problem with providing a number is that this is summative. It does not identify strengths and weaknesses or provide feedback for learning and development.

John Hattie (2009), in his seminal work, *Visible Learning*, identifies the importance of feedback. His meta-research, which brings together hundreds of pieces of education research, indicates that timely, appropriate, and learner-focused feedback is one of the most significant things that we can provide our students to improve their learning outcomes. Jody Nyquist (2003) further identifies that knowledge of results—what a student scores in the assessment—is the weakest form of feedback; the strongest feedback consists of knowledge of results, an explanation, and an immediate activity to bridge the gap.

The shift that needs to occur to provide such feedback and opportunities is simple to explain but requires mindfulness to implement. Let's look at an example and improve on it. Consider, for example, a teacher who returns a marked quiz to the student that includes a simple number such as 7/10. Now let's reimagine this example with mindful shifts.

The teacher prepares an activity with specific questions and specific activities to reinforce the learning for each question if the students' response to the questions shows the activity is required. Then, one of the following approaches transpires.

- The students mark the quizzes themselves and then individually undertake the learning activity that reinforces the identified area of weakness.
- The students mark the quizzes and identify which activities are needed, and then form learning groups to complete the activities identified.

- Instead of a quiz, the teacher presents the questions one at a time, and the students attempt the answer. The students then break into groups in which at least one member understood the concept. They work collaboratively on the activity to reduce the gap, supported by their peers. The teacher presents the next question, and new groups are assembled.

These are mindful shifts that transform a simple quiz into a rich, collaborative learning activity. Teachers can apply these shifts to instruction and assessment throughout all stages of learning. As Nyquist (2003) states, this practice constitutes strong feedback, as there is knowledge of the correct results and an explanation with an activity to bridge the gap. Further, as the students are also helping to lead the learning process, this reinforces their own learning.

# The Learning Process

Michael Stevenson (2007), vice president of global education at Cisco, describes the learning process in three stages: (1) knowledge acquisition, (2) knowledge deepening, and finally (3) knowledge creation. This progression aligns well with Benjamin S. Bloom's work (1956), and subsequently Lorin W. Anderson and David Krathwohl's (2001), in the development of the cognitive domain of Bloom's taxonomy (see chapter 2 for a closer examination of Bloom's taxonomic levels). Knowledge acquisition occurs through Bloom's *lower-order thinking skills* (LOTS) of remembering and understanding. As a student is able to analyze and apply these concepts, the knowledge deepens. When the student is finally able to take this knowledge and use it to evaluate and create knowledge, he or she has reached the *higher-order thinking skills* (HOTS). See figure 1.1 for an illustration of how these skills align within the learning process's three stages.

Note that the most advanced stage of the learning process, knowledge creation, intersects with the highest taxonomic levels, creating and evaluating. Further, knowledge creation accounts for the triangle's largest portion. This is because HOTS depend on and build on the development of LOTS. Figure 1.1 illustrates that each stage of learning grows larger with the newly developed knowledge. It is for this reason that our work with schools focuses primarily on evaluation and creation. Starting at the top incorporates everything below automatically.

At each stage (acquisition, deepening, and creation) of the learning process, we can apply the different assessment types (diagnostic, formative, and summative) and their alignment to different assessment objectives and outcomes (see table 1.1, page 12). Diagnostic assessment provides us with a starting point to begin the learning journey. It indicates and begins to activate students' prior knowledge and experience. Diagnostic assessment is a time saver that prevents reteaching concepts students already understand or backtracking to cover the basics that have been missed or forgotten. It sets the starting point

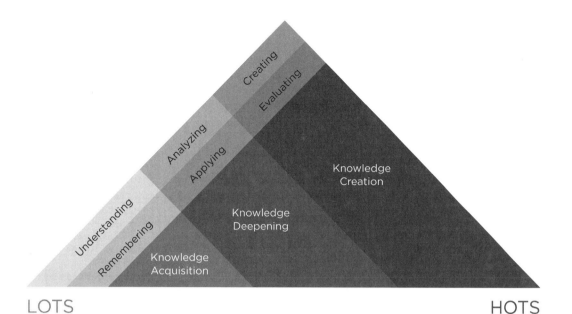

**Figure 1.1: Stages of learning.**

and checks the current position on the learning journey. Diagnostic assessment is looking back and preparing forward. In simple terms, diagnostic assessment is assessment *for* learning, to ascertain what learners are already capable of in order to best determine what needs to be taught. Formative assessment is sometimes referred to as assessment *as* learning (Broadfoot et al., 2002). The formative feedback cycle allows students to test their understanding and gather timely and appropriate learning and learner-centric feedback in order to adjust or correct their understanding and move their learning forward. It is the natural learning process described previously in everything we do, from teaching a child to cook to mastering a martial art—measured, learning-centered feedback followed by the opportunity to try again. Summative assessment is assessment *of* learning at a specific moment in time.

Any assessment task can be used diagnostically, formatively, or summatively. It is how the task is applied that determines this. For example, criterion-based assessments, like the rubrics for the fluencies you'll encounter in chapters 3–8, are well designed for formative assessment, as they not only identify where a learner is, but also where they should aim to improve. Through gap analysis, a learner and teacher can determine the next steps they need to take to close the gap, making the assessment formative. However, assigning a simple one, two, three, or four, without the opportunity to discuss, revise, and improve, makes criterion-based assessment summative. As we have noted, this book argues for formative assessment use over summative assessment. As summative assessment only reflects learning, does not provide opportunities to extend or enhance understanding, and is not the best representation of overall learning, it falls outside

**Table 1.1: Assessment Types**

| Assessment Type | **Diagnostic** | **Formative** | **Summative** |
| --- | --- | --- | --- |
| | Looking back<br><br>Preparing forward | Looking back and preparing forward<br><br>Feeding back and feeding forward | Feeding back<br><br>Providing a snapshot |
| **Assessment Objectives and Outcomes** | **Assessment *for* Learning** | **Assessment *as* Learning** | **Assessment *of* Learning** |
| | Ascertaining students' prior knowledge, perceptions, and misconceptions; monitoring student learning progress; and informing teaching practice and curriculum planning in order to support students' future learning and understanding | Focusing on constructive feedback from the teacher and on developing students' capacity to self-assess and to reflect on their learning to improve their future learning and understanding | Making judgments about what the student has learned in relation to the teaching and learning goals; should be comprehensive and reflect the learning growth over the time period being assessed |

*Source: Adapted from Holmes-Smith, 2005; Stevenson, 2007.*

the book's scope, and we will not discuss summative assessment in detail. We have, however, included it in table 1.1 to illustrate how it compares with other assessment types.

In the following sections, we will discuss the diagnostic and formative assessments' roles within the learning process and examine some of the practical forms these assessments can take.

# Diagnostic Assessment

Teachers use diagnostic assessment to identify the strengths and weaknesses in a student's understanding. As Paul Black, Chris Harrison, Clara Lee, Bethan Marshall, and Dylan Wiliam (2003) state, it is used to provide information about what a teacher should do next to improve his or her students' learning. Diagnostic assessment also allows the teacher to develop an understanding of his or her current situation and enables effective planning, including access to resources, support, and timing adjustments (see figure 1.2).

Most often, we will see and use diagnostic assessment at the start of a learning process, be it the start of a unit to diagnose prior learning, skills, and processes, or the start of a lesson to assess the understanding and synthesis of the prior lesson's material.

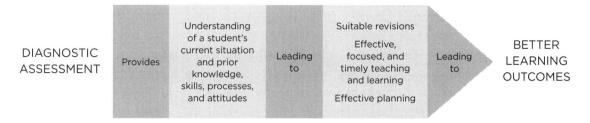

**Figure 1.2: Diagnostic assessment outcomes.**

There are several pieces of information that are critical when starting a journey. Destination is the most obvious, but not necessarily the most important. When we travel, many of us invest a lot of time in researching our destination to gain the most from our experience. We also invest considerable time and energy in deciding the route we'll take to get there. But is it fair to say we seldom consider our starting point? We take point A for granted. Many of our decisions in planning for our trip are based on our starting point, and yet we rarely give it much thought.

Now, imagine you are on a game show, dropped into an unknown location, and told that you have to make your way to the end to win a prize. "Where am I?" is the first question that comes to mind. You could start off in what you perceive as the correct direction, based on your assumptions. However, this approach may lead to lengthy delays as you encounter unexpected obstacles, dead ends, and potential disaster! This could cost you the race and the prize. Suddenly, where you start becomes very important. Most of us would, in this situation, invest some time to identify our current position to accurately and efficiently plot our course. Spending the time to take stock of your situation before you run off in search of the prize is going to start you off on the right foot and ensure you don't run into trouble en route.

Children entering school have markedly different cognitive, language, emotional, social, and psychomotor development levels. These gaps in areas of learning and development persist throughout the years of school and beyond (Masters, 2013). And so, just as in the game show, in education it's important to identify each student's starting point, rather than make assumptions about his or her prior knowledge and experience, thus avoiding missed learning opportunities and time spent focusing on activities that he or she already understands and has synthesized. This will also reveal potential misunderstandings that teachers must correct to enable students to properly develop and mature in their learning. Many factors determine their varying starting points, including their prior educational experiences and maturity levels. No two students are alike, and the basis for their learning is just as varied.

Our awareness of these differences is critical to effective teaching and learning. In *Educational Psychology: A Cognitive View*, David P. Ausubel and colleagues say, "If I had to reduce all of educational psychology to just one principle, I would say this: The most important single factor influencing learning is what the learner already knows. Ascertain this and teach him accordingly" (Ausubel, Novak, & Hanesian, 1978, p. 163). In *Understanding by Design, Second Edition*, Grant Wiggins and Jay McTighe (2005) also stress this idea, essentially stating that successful educational design requires you, the teacher or learning leader, to do the following.

- Know where you are.

- Know where you want to be.

- Know how you are going to measure the gap.

From here, you can do a gap analysis that indicates the distance between your existing position and your desired destination. A gap analysis is the difference between where you want to be (your learning outcomes and goals) and where you are (your diagnostic assessment). Once you have established where you want to go and where you are, you can design the pathway or route to reach your educational endpoints.

## Deliberate and Purposeful Assessment

Diagnostic assessment is a tool for use during class to quickly gain information about the students' understanding of the concept they are examining and how we as classroom practitioners are facilitating learning. Dominic Wyse, Louise Hayward, and Jessica Pandya (2015) state, "Assessment procedures should include explicit processes to ensure that information is valid and is as reliable as necessary for its purpose" (p. 35). In other words, all assessments should be deliberate and purposeful. In developing a diagnostic assessment that meets these criteria, no matter what form it will take, we must consider a number of factors prior to developing the questions.

- **Identify the assumed knowledge, processes, or skills:** This consists of knowledge, skills, or processes that we expect students to have already learned. Well-designed curricula are developed as a series of progressions that build on the prior learning. These spiral curricula will see students revisit related concepts as they progress and mature in the schooling system. It is vital that the students and teacher have a deep and rich understanding of the preceding year's learning and a matching understanding of the next year's syllabus.

- **Identify the base elements of the current unit of learning:** Recognizing the students' understanding of their current work is a critical part of diagnostic testing. Often students have more depth of knowledge, experience, and understanding than teachers expect. For students who already have deep knowledge, being taught the content again demotivates and disengages them. A teacher who administers diagnostic testing can make informed decisions about the starting point for the learning journey and about how to differentiate learning to accommodate the students with detailed prior learning or deficits in their expected learning.

- **Decide on the assessment method:** The choice of assessment method is vital and will vary from unit to unit and subject to subject. The learners' age will also critically influence the choice. The method must suit the audience and the purpose. Teachers must also consider the time available to assess the students' prior and existing learning.

Once we consider these items, we can then develop the diagnostic tasks or questions. Each question we write or task we develop must be deliberate and purposeful. For each and every question or part of the diagnostic task, we must ask the following questions.

- What does this question or task examine?

- Does it accurately identify existing knowledge?

- Can it help differentiate the different depths of knowledge, skills, or processes?

- What is the correct answer?

- How can I use it to improve learning?

Once we have developed the diagnostic assessment, we must then ask ourselves the following two fundamental questions.

1. **Is it suitable for the audience?** It is easy to write questions and tasks that we as educators can understand, but these may be difficult for our developing learners to comprehend. It is always advisable to have a fellow teacher read through your diagnostic assessment or to use online reading-level tools like the SMOG (simple measure of gobbledygook) index. *SMOG* is a formula that analyzes a writing's complexity and therefore readability. Visit https://readability-score.com/text to access a free online readability tool using the SMOG index. (Visit **go.SolutionTree.com/assessment** to access live links to the websites mentioned in this book.)

2. **Is it suitable for the purpose?** The purpose is to determine the level of prior knowledge that the students possess for a topic of learning.

## *Forms of Diagnostic Assessment*

Short written tests and multiple-choice questions are frequently used diagnostic assessments. In developing a broad understanding of the students' knowledge, these are viable and effective assessments that teachers can administer and mark quickly and, when well designed, can provide indicative information about the student's knowledge and diagnostically assess a student's recall and understanding for a particular subject.

The following are some guidelines for writing effective multiple-choice questions to diagnose prior learning of concepts or theory. The examples we have chosen are based on materials from the Learning Management Corporation (n.d.).

- **Keep it simple:** Try to remove extra reading which may be confusing or distract from the questions.

  - Good example—Food travelling through the digestive tract passes from the stomach to the _____.
    - a. epiglottis
    - b. esophagus
    - c. large intestine
    - d. small intestine

  - Bad example—Food travelling through the digestive tract passes from the stomach, a large muscular sac that produces acid located directly under the diaphragm, to the _____.
    - a. small intestine
    - b. large intestine
    - c. esophagus
    - d. epiglottis

  Don't provide information that you could use later in the assessment. Watch out for grammatical clues that may give away the correct answer. Make sure you have only one correct answer but that your other answers are plausible.

- **Avoid negatives:** Avoid using negatives like *not* in the questions.

  - Good example—Which of the following is located near the mouth?
    - a. epiglottis
    - b. large intestine
    - c. small intestine
    - d. stomach

  - Bad example—Which of the following is not in the abdominal cavity?
    - a. small intestine
    - b. large intestine
    - c. epiglottis
    - d. stomach

- **Organize your questions:** Arrange your answers alphabetically, in increasing size (numerical order), or in time sequence. Present your answers vertically, as this is easier to read than horizontally.

  - Good example—Which organ produces acid to digest food?

    a.  epiglottis

    b.  large intestine

    c.  small intestine

    d.  stomach

  - Bad example—Which organ produces acid to digest food?

    a.  small intestine

    b.  large intestine

    c.  epiglottis

    d.  stomach

By considering and carefully structuring diagnostic assessment, mindful teachers are able to determine the depth of student understanding. They avoid the pitfalls of leading questions or questions that are structured in such a manner that they are hard to read or understand, and they focus assessment on determining prior knowledge and learning.

However, written tests are not the only mechanism that teachers can use to determine the student's understanding, knowledge, and skills. The following is an assessment that does not take the form of a traditional written-answer test.

General science is one of the subjects that Andrew teaches. Within the science curriculum in the living world strand, there is a requirement to understand the processes of life. This unpacks into developing an understanding of nutrition and digestion. Many students may be able to name parts of the digestive tract but lack the depth of understanding to make accurate representations of the various organs' sizes or how they interconnect.

To determine the depth of their understanding and therefore provide Andrew with a starting point for the series of lessons, the class—working in pairs or small groups—constructs a life-size drawing of the human digestive system and attempts to accurately label the parts.

The process works like this. One student lies flat on a large sheet of butcher paper, and his or her peers draw a rough outline of the torso, head, and limbs, tracing around the student. The students then make a list of all the parts of the human digestive tract that they can recall and proceed to draw these into the outline on the paper. The students are asked to consider the sequence of the organs, the relative size and position, and if they can remember organs' roles or features, and add these details to the diagram. The task is usually tackled with enthusiasm and a fair amount of laughter. For Andrew as the teacher, observing the groups as they work, he can quickly ascertain the depth and accuracy of their knowledge and adjust the starting point of the learning sequence accordingly. He collects the diagrams for later reference. Andrew will repeat this task at the end of the teaching sequence, and then return the original models to the students so they can see the progress they have made.

This task is diagnostic in that it provides a clear understanding of students' prior knowledge and enables Andrew to tailor students' learning experience to suit their needs. It is also formative, as the students can receive feedback while Andrew walks around the room, observing and discussing this learning task.

Such activities help a teacher ascertain students' starting points of knowledge or their current level of understanding. Once teachers have a firm understanding of their students' current states, they can move toward planning formative assessments.

# Formative Assessment

Planning and preparation are essential in all formative assessment methods. Providing quality formative assessment requires a depth of relevant knowledge of the concepts, principles, processes, or procedures involved in the assessed learning. Understanding the criteria, as well as the ability to apply them, is critical to providing focused and relevant feedback and evaluation. In other words, if you don't understand the lesson being assessed, you can't provide relevant help and support.

Benjamin S. Bloom (1956) was one of the first educational theorists to recognize formative assessment, or as he called it, formative evaluation. He theorized and applied this concept to provide feedback and corrections at all stages in the teaching and learning process. Paul Black and Dylan Wiliam, in their 1998 article "Assessment and Classroom Learning," define formative assessment as "encompassing all those activities undertaken by teachers, and/or by their students, which provide information to be used as feedback to modify the teaching and learning activities in which they are engaged" (p. 7). In short, formative assessment is a task or activity that provides learners an opportunity to receive evaluation or feedback from themselves, their peers, or their instructor to enhance and support their learning.

While in many education systems, formative assessment has not yet caught on to reflect evolving curricula and standards, it is mandated in others. For instance, New South Wales (NSW) Department of Education and Training (2008b) in Australia states in its publication *Principles of Assessment and Reporting in NSW Public Schools*:

- Assessment should be integrated into the teaching and learning cycle.

- Assessment needs to be an ongoing, integral part of the teaching and learning cycle. It must allow teachers and students themselves to monitor learning. From the teacher perspective, it provides the evidence to guide the next steps in teaching and learning.

- From the student perspective, it provides the opportunity to reflect on and review progress, and can provide the motivation and direction for further learning.

Formative assessment can be formal or informal, spontaneous or scheduled. It can be as simple as an impromptu question and answer between student and teacher as the teacher moves around the classroom, or it can be a more structured and formalized event. For example, students could offer examples of their work for critique to both teachers and peers to provide evaluation and feedback, which they could maintain within a portfolio. Similarly, teachers can implement it as an assessment against a criterion, with the teacher providing indications of how to improve against this descriptor. No matter how teachers implement formative assessment, it provides the learner with an opportunity to engage with feedback and make corrections as learning progresses.

While teachers often facilitate formative assessment opportunities, feedback is not exclusively their domain. The learners themselves and their peers often provide the most frequent formative feedback. In the following sections, we will examine students' self-reflection and feedback from teachers and peers. We will then take a close look at one of the most effective instruments for employing formative assessment: the student portfolio.

Teachers should encourage students to self-question and to self-verbalize their performance. Self-questioning and self-verbalizing are metacognitive strategies in which the student creates appropriate questions, then predicts the answers, validates these answers, and then summarizes them. John Hattie (2012) notes that self-verbalization and self-questioning have a significant impact and that student expectations and self-reported grades have the highest effect size of all the factors he analyzed that influence achievement.

When students are considering their own performance, a useful framework comes from Australian educators. Education departments across Australia have widely used Stephen Dinham's (2008a) research regarding powerful teacher feedback. Dinham notes that in formative assessment, the mindful educators and students ask and answer three key questions.

1. What can I do?

2. What can't I do?

3. How can I do better?

These first two questions are feedback on what the student can or cannot do in regards to a stated goal. It is learner and learning focused, appropriate, honest, and supportive. It needs to be timely to have any relevance. Feedback, no matter how detailed, delivered a month after the fact is hardly relevant. The third question is empowering: How can I do better? What do I need to do to improve?

A further question is sometimes added to these three key questions: how does my work compare with that of others? This is a challenging question. Should I know where I am in the class? Will this help me? How will it make others feel? We know that a degree of competition is useful and important. This is a question that you have the students ask only when you have a very good relationship with the class, and is dependent on the students' maturity and age.

John Hattie and Helen Timperley (2007) propose a model of reflection to enhance learning as well. Their model is slightly simpler than Dinham's (2008a) and has the students address three questions.

1. Where am I going? (the goals)

2. How am I going? (the progress)

3. Where to next? (activities for improvement)

While both models are similar, Hattie and Timperley's is more goal or task focused, whereas Dinham's is more general.

# High-Quality Feedback

*Source: An earlier version of the material in this section appears in Churches, n.d. Used with permission.*

Feedback is a crucial component of mindful assessment and is the heart of formative assessment. Hattie's (2012) findings from his meta-analysis of hundreds of education research papers indicate that providing formative evaluation and feedback has some of the largest effects on student learning. For an assessment to be formative, students must be receptive to the feedback and use it to adjust their learning. In order to ensure this receptiveness, there must be a relationship between the recipient and the assessor based on trust, mutual goals and objectives, and shared purpose. Without an established, trusting, and respectful relationship, teachers and students are unlikely to find the feedback, with its critical aspects, authoritative or learner centric. Hattie (2012) identifies the importance of the teacher-student relationship along with teacher credibility. He notes that there must be a relationship of trust between the learner and the learning leader for feedback to be effective. Should the learner not have trust and faith in the instructor, he or she will struggle to take the advice and critique offered. Feedback can be a hard pill to swallow; we all struggle to accept critique and find it uncomfortable. A positive, affirming, and honest relationship between both parties is necessary to enable this dialogue.

Similarly, feedback from peers requires trust and understanding as well as clear ground rules for behavior, process, and so on. A student's observation, consideration, and critique of another's work can often be beneficial to his or her own work. The student will consider the aspects of his or her peer's performance, processes, or products and use this reflection to enhance his or her own learning.

Without feedback, assessment is not a learning activity; it is a compliance task. Feedback, whether from the teacher or instructor or from peers, must be all of the following (Churches, n.d.).

- **Timely:** Students cannot learn, change, and develop if the unit has ended when they receive their feedback. We must provide feedback often and in detail during the process.

- **Appropriate and reflective:** Feedback must reflect the students' ability, maturity, and age. It must be understandable. Different learners mature at different rates, so feedback should be an individualized process based on each student's social and intellectual maturity.

- **Honest and supportive:** Feedback can be devastating to a student who has invested a considerable amount of time and energy into a task. Receiving a critique that identifies weaknesses of one's work can be very disheartening. We must provide feedback that is both honest and supportive. The feedback must provide encouragement to continue and guidance on how to achieve the desired goals.

- **Focused on learning and linked to the task's purpose:** The feedback needs to be descriptive. It should also link to the big picture as well as the specific aspects being assessed. Again looking at Hattie's (2012) research, teacher clarity has a high effect score in the list of influences on achievement—the clarity and descriptive nature of the feedback the teacher presents are major influences.

- **Enabling:** Receiving feedback without the opportunity to act on it is frustrating, limiting, and counterproductive. Students must be able to learn from the formative assessments and apply the feedback and corrections.

Nyquist (2003) developed the Model of Effective Feedback, which is one of the better models for providing feedback in a higher education setting, but it matches well with all education levels. Essentially, the Model of Effective Feedback has five stages that increase in strength (Churches, n.d.).

1. **Knowledge of results (KoR):** Weak or poor feedback occurs when students receive feedback containing only the knowledge of their results. This could be a test score or a letter grade for an assignment, report, or task. The learners have knowledge of their relative success in the task but do not know how to improve on it or where they went wrong. This is what often happens

with final examinations. The students receive their final grade, but they have no opportunity to develop or learn.

2. **Knowledge of correct results (KCR):** This stage develops from the previous stage. Here the teacher gives students their KoR as well as KCR. For example, students receive their completed exams and the teacher works through the correct responses with the class. The learners can see the differences between their answers and the correct ones, but there is no explanation as to why the answers were either right or wrong, nor is there any follow-up activity to this exercise.

   As you can imagine, just reading out the correct answers is not particularly useful. This is still weak feedback but better than just giving students a grade. There is some opportunity to learn, but it is limited and dependent on the learners' initiative to instigate self-directed learning and inquiry. KoR and KCR are essentially auditing techniques.

3. **Knowledge of correct results and explanation (KCR+e):** If the teacher takes the time to explain the difference between student results (KoR) and the correct answers (KCR), this stage of feedback is much more powerful. Here learners can begin to understand and clarify the differences between what they undertook and what the expectations were. We call this knowledge of correct results plus explanation (KCR+e).

4. **KCR+e and specific actions to reduce the gap:** The next stage continues the logical progression. The students know their results and the correct answer. The teacher now explains the difference between the two and gives them specific actions they can take to reduce the gap.

5. **KCR+e and activity:** The teacher provides students with KCR+e and specific actions to reduce the gap, as well as an activity that reinforces the processes, skills, concepts, or learning.

Figure 1.3 illustrates the stages' hierarchy.

The teacher who provides either KCR+e and a specific action or ideally KCR+e and an immediate activity gives the learner the best opportunity to maximize learning, and the teacher has achieved the clearest picture of his or her students' levels of learning. One of the best ways to document this process of increased learning and provide opportunities for further reflection is through student portfolios.

There has been much talk of portfolios and portfolio-based assessment, along with a great deal of confusion (Gronlund, 1998; Wiggins, 1990). Much of the confusion comes from misunderstanding what a portfolio is. Many think of an artist's portfolio as a collection of his or her best works. But such a collection would really be more of an exhibition than a portfolio. We hold a picture in our minds of the artist sitting in front

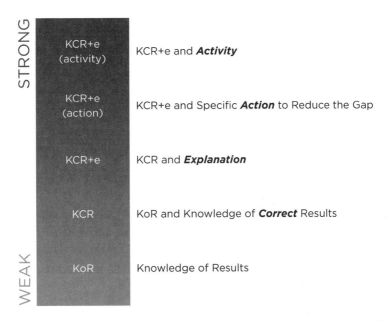

**STRONG**

KCR+e
(activity) — KCR+e and *Activity*

KCR+e
(action) — KCR+e and Specific *Action* to Reduce the Gap

KCR+e — KCR and *Explanation*

KCR — KoR and Knowledge of *Correct* Results

KoR — Knowledge of Results

**WEAK**

**Figure 1.3: Levels of Nyquist's (2003) Model of Effective Feedback.**

of a canvas and bursting forth with a creative masterpiece. But this romantic notion is far from the process's reality.

The logical, methodical, and chronicled process that leads to the development of a work may appear to be the opposite of what we envision as the creative process, but it is not. Most of Leonardo da Vinci's famous works are not the final paintings but the sketches and drawings that were notes on his research into anatomy and a multitude of other subjects. The point is that a portfolio is a record of the development of one's thinking and ideas—a record that provides background to the finished product.

This not only allows for formative assessment, but also clearly demonstrates the formation of ideas and understandings that teachers cannot adequately measure in any other way. It is one of the reasons that assessment must move away from externally mandated standardized testing and back into educators' hands. They are truly the only ones who are in a position to adequately assess a learner's progress.

Regarding application in the classroom, blogging sites and various types of software can be used. Blogging sites like WordPress (https://wordpress.org) or school-hosted blogging software (http://edublogs.org) are often used as portfolio tools. Students post blog entries to present their work and then invite comments from their peers or instructor. Blogging tools are versatile enough to allow either the teacher to set up and moderate the students' posts and comments or to enable the blogger to control who has access to his or her work portfolio. Teachers at Wilderness School in Adelaide, Australia, have recently used iBooks for this process. Students chronicle their work, chapter by chapter, and submit the finished book as evidence not only of learning but of the learning process.

There are also software packages that enable this controlled and structured conversation between the learner and the learner's critical friends to occur. In New Zealand, the Tertiary Education Commission in conjunction with a number of prominent tertiary education providers developed the open source ePortfolio system Mahara (https:// mahara.org) as a learner-centered personal learning environment. This product is widely used around the world.

Mindfulness should be at the root of assessment that addresses each stage of learning, from higher-order skills to lower-order skills. Diagnostic assessments that provide teachers with information about students' prior knowledge and starting points, and formative assessments that simultaneously reflect what students are learning and provide opportunities to extend that learning are essential for teaching and assessing the skills students need for success in the 21st century. In the next chapter, we examine the building blocks of the framework for assessing these skills.

# Guiding Questions

Before moving to the next chapter, answer the following questions as an individual or with your school team.

1. What does it mean to be mindful?

2. What are the purposes of assessment?

3. Why has summative assessment been the norm in our education system for so long?

4. What is the most effective method of assessing learning?

5. How does assessment align with 21st century students and innovative learning environments?

6. How can we become mindful about how we assess student learning?

# chapter 2

# Structure of the Fluencies Assessment Framework

There are two main factors we considered while developing the fluencies assessment framework: (1) the skills our students need and (2) how these skills can be measured. As the preface to this book notes, the essential fluencies identify a number of distinct skills that students need for success in the 21st century. We arrived at these skills by observing trends in the developing global economy, which align strongly with Daniel H. Pink's (2005) observations of the global economic challenges he attributes to the 3As—(1) Asia, (2) automation, and (3) abundance—which he argues will be major influences for our workforce in the future.

Many companies have largely outsourced or offshored routine physical work, such as that performed on an assembly line, to factories in Asia that are capable of hiring and onboarding thousands of workers in a single day to be ready for work the following day and at a fraction of the price of similar workers in North America. Asia, automation, and abundance will shape our education as well as society itself with respect to not only what we learn but more importantly how we learn. Schools will focus more on activities and less on subjects. Therefore, the ways in which we assess students will also need to change.

The essential fluencies are our answer to the driving question, How can we teach the essential skills our curricula identify in a structured manner? There has been a rapid adoption of these and similar processes worldwide, which has created a demand for considering their assessment. If we measure what we know matters, then what will matter is more than what is measured now. The question we most often hear is, How do we assess these processes? As educators, we know that we must lead the process and we must be able to measure our students' journey. The essential fluencies cannot be completely measured with traditional summative assessment—nor should they be. Such an assessment measures only an outcome. The fluencies are not an outcome but something to continually develop throughout a person's life. As we discussed in the preceding chapter, we must identify students' knowledge through diagnostic assessment and further cultivate it with formative assessments. With these methods as a basis, we have developed an assessment framework and rubrics for teachers to apply when assessing the essential fluencies, which we will outline in this chapter. It is important that teachers embed these methods in the foundation of their use of these frameworks and tools.

# Phases of the Assessment Framework

In designing our assessment framework, we identified four distinct phases that students move through as they apply different types of skills at different complexity levels within their learning. These phases correspond directly to four-level rubrics we've developed to facilitate evaluation, which we illustrate later in this chapter. When examining students' performance in relation to these phases, it's important for teachers to keep in mind that measurement of the fluencies involves measuring the development of a person *over time*—the incremental improvements that take place. The taxonomic levels that Bloom's (1956) cognitive domain outlines provide a guide for identifying these improvements.

Bloom (1956) describes three domains of learning: (1) *psychomotor*—describing manual and physical skills and acquisition, (2) *affective*—dealing with attitudes, emotions, and feelings, and (3) *cognitive*—dealing with processing information and knowledge and the development of mental skills. It is this cognitive domain that educators are most familiar with. Bloom's taxonomy is represented by the following taxonomic levels in this domain, arranged from LOTS to HOTS.

- **Remembering:** Retrieving, recalling, or recognizing knowledge from memory; when learners use memory to produce definitions, facts, or lists, or to recite or retrieve material

- **Understanding:** Constructing meaning from different types of functions, be they written or graphic

- **Applying:** Carrying out or using a procedure through executing or implementing; relates and refers to situations in which students use learned material through products such as models, presentations, interviews, and simulations

- **Analyzing:** Breaking material or concepts into parts, determining how the parts relate or interrelate to one another or to an overall structure or purpose; mental actions include differentiating, organizing, and attributing as well as being able to distinguish between components

- **Evaluating:** Making judgments based on criteria and standards through checking and critiquing

- **Creating:** Putting the elements together to form a coherent or functional whole; reorganizing elements into a new pattern or structure through generating, planning, or producing

In innovative learning, students use higher-order thinking to create products as solutions to relevant real-world problems. We have always stressed that creating relevance for the learner is the educator's first responsibility and that without it learning will not occur. We focus on relevance for this reason. To this end, in structuring our assessment framework, we include the elements *awareness* and *connection* in an amended Bloom's taxonomy to clearly illustrate relevance's importance.

Awareness is quite obviously necessary at the beginning of the learning process, as learners cannot remember something of which they are not aware. They first must have awareness of its existence. We might describe connection in the context of relevance to learners, but it is also their level of curiosity, engagement with the stimulus material, perceived value of the information, and desire to know more.

As facilitators of learning, we must focus on creating awareness and stimulating connection, as these have the most impact on the potential for and depth of learning. For reflective teachers and administrators, we suggest considering the depth of connection to learning educators create in their lessons as part of a formative conversation in unit revision and potentially teacher evaluations.

Once entering our consciousness through awareness, connection becomes the critical factor that determines which of Bloom's taxonomic levels the learning has the potential to reach. If there is a low level of connection, we can at best hope that learners will achieve remembering or understanding. Conversely, a high level of connection can drive the learning to the heights of evaluating and even creating. Adding awareness and connection therefore provides the foundation for learning in the four distinct phases of the essential fluencies assessment framework. Figure 2.1 (page 28) illustrates how Bloom's amended taxonomy informs the structure and phases of the framework for assessing the fluencies.

We arrange these eight taxonomic levels within four framework phases for several reasons. Four phases is, quite simply, a manageable number, and we find that assigning more than four phases to evaluate students would be unnecessarily difficult. Adding rubric levels beyond the four we've outlined here is also impractical and counterproductive; there is no reason to add multiple levels of failure within a rubric.

In addition to the foundational skills of connection and awareness, remembering is also a fundamental skill; these three, therefore, comprise phase 1. Remembering is completely different from understanding, the next highest-thinking skill, so phase 2 begins with understanding. As understanding and applying require similar thought processes, they are both assigned to phase 2. There is a natural division between applying (phase 2) and analyzing (phase 3), as the two skills are fundamentally different. Analyzing and evaluating, however, are taxonomic levels that go hand in hand, so we have grouped these skills into phase 3. Finally, creating is completely different from analyzing, and the most complex thinking is required to perform this skill, so we have

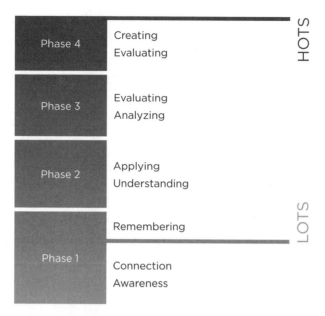

**Figure 2.1: Alignment of Bloom's taxonomic levels with assessment phases for the essential fluencies.**

assigned it to the highest phase: phase 4. Note that in cases where creating is not applicable within the skill being measured, evaluation is assigned to phase 4, as it is not only the highest level achievable but also separate from analysis.

For this framework's structure, we have purposely chosen universally applicable phases as opposed to a grade-level approach, as proficiency with the fluencies is irrespective of age. Kindergarten students, for example, can have the capacity to reach the highest levels in consideration of their developmental maturation, and we frequently see this occur. While it might be within a limited scope of experiences and not at the depth we see at a more senior level, they can still perform HOTS. Although we developed the framework irrespective of age, teachers should apply it with age-appropriate expectations. This approach also aligns with the assessment practices of the International Baccalaureate Primary Years Programme and Middle Years Programme (www.ibo.org), the New Zealand Curriculum framework (http://nzcurriculum.tki.org.nz), and many more.

# Criterion-Based Assessment Tools

Criterion-based tools such as rubrics provide a series of descriptors to accurately measure and describe a student's learning. These are helpful tools for assessment that progress from no knowledge to a comprehensive understanding and application of the process or aspect being examined. They are the basis for the tools we have created to help teachers identify student achievement levels for the fluencies, which we provide in later chapters. See figures 3.1–3.6 (pages 47–54), 4.1–4.5 (pages 67–72), 5.1–5.5

(pages 83–87), 6.1–6.2 (pages 96–98), 7.1–7.5 (pages 111–117), and 8.1–8.5 (pages 128–138). In this section, we will outline ideal rubric function, elements, and creation. Note that we prefer to avoid language identifying the student in rubrics, as it turns it into a judgment of the individual and not the work. "The student provided little research" has a completely different tone than "The work includes little research." Let's keep feedback focused on the work and not the person. See figure 2.2 for an example of a typical rubric students may encounter.

| 1 | 2 | 3 | 4 |
|---|---|---|---|
| The work states a concept. | The work outlines a concept. | The work describes a concept. | The work explains a concept. |

**Figure 2.2: Basic rubric.**

Often, assessments present students with two challenges. The first is understanding what the examiner is asking, and the second is the question itself. If students fail to understand the former, it is highly unlikely that they will be able to demonstrate their synthesis of the assessment task. In other words, if they don't understand the assessment, they have little chance of being successful. To illustrate this point in workshops, we start with just this simple rubric shown in figure 2.2, and ask teachers to define success criteria for each phase. Usually, in these settings, there is a great deal of difficulty reaching any kind of consensus. This comes from not having clear definitions of command terms. It is essential that there is an understanding among all team members of the terms' meanings and what is required to demonstrate success.

## Common Language of Assessment

Having a common language of assessment that both learners and their teachers clearly understand removes the first barrier to assessment. A common language of assessment provides transparency and fairness as well as a simple structure with which to mark the tasks.

Inherent in this process must be an understanding of the command terms—in the case of figure 2.2, these are *state, outline, describe,* and *explain*—and what they reflect. Many examination or assessment systems include definitions of commonly used command terms. To ensure clarity and fairness, a school or district should develop and adopt a standard set of definitions for command terms and provide these to all stakeholders. Teachers should then develop assessments and evidence statements using this common language and can provide the definitions to students at the beginning of the year or include them with each assessment.

The command terms' sequence is critical and links to Bloom's taxonomy, moving from LOTS to HOTS. As such, it also correlates with the four phases for assessing the fluencies. For example, *state* is a function of remembering, *describe* and *explain* are functions of understanding, and so on.

Because technology has so profoundly influenced our lives and student lives since the original publication of Bloom's taxonomy in 1956, and even since Anderson and Krathwohl's (2001) revision of it, table 2.1 shows our digital taxonomy, which identifies specific technology-related skills and actions that align with each of Bloom's taxonomic levels. We list them in gerund form to allow teachers to easily identify the performance of these skills and actions for the purpose of assessment.

**Table 2.1: Bloom's Digital Taxonomy Verbs**

| Remembering | Understanding | Applying | Analyzing | Evaluating | Creating |
|---|---|---|---|---|---|
| Bookmarking | Advanced searching | Acting out | Advertising | Arguing | Adapting |
| Bullet pointing | Annotating | Administering | Appraising | Assessing | Animating |
| Copying | Associating | Applying | Attributing | Checking | Blogging |
| Defining | Boolean searching | Articulating | Breaking down | Commenting | Building |
| Describing | Categorizing | Calculating | Calculating | Concluding | Collaborating |
| Duplicating | Classifying | Carrying out | Categorizing | Considering | Composing |
| Favoriting | Commenting | Changing | Classifying | Convincing | Constructing |
| Finding | Comparing | Charting | Comparing | Criticizing | Designing |
| Googling | Conducting | Choosing | Concluding | Critiquing | Developing |
| Highlighting | Contrasting | Collecting | Contrasting | Debating | Devising |
| Identifying | Converting | Completing | Correlating | Defending | Directing |
| Labeling | Demonstrating | Computing | Deconstructing | Detecting | Facilitating |
| Liking | Describing | Constructing | Deducing | Editorializing | Filming |
| Listening | Differentiating | Demonstrating | Differentiating | Experimenting | Formulating |
| Listing | Discovering | Determining | Discriminating | Grading | Integrating |
| Locating | Discussing | Displaying | Distinguishing | Hypothesizing | Inventing |
| Matching | Distinguishing | Editing | Dividing | Judging | Leading |
| Memorizing | Estimating | Examining | Estimating | Justifying | Making |
| Naming | Exemplifying | Executing | Explaining | Measuring | Managing |
| Networking | Explaining | Experimenting | Illustrating | Moderating | Mixing and remixing |
| Numbering | Expressing | Explaining | Inferring | Monitoring | Modifying |
| Quoting | Extending | Hacking | Integrating | Networking | Negotiating |
| Reading | Gathering | Implementing | Linking | Persuading | Orating |
| Recalling | Generalizing | Interviewing | Mashing | Posting | Originating |
| Reciting | Grouping | Judging | Mind mapping | Predicting | Planning |
| Recognizing | Identifying | Loading | Ordering | Rating | Podcasting |
| Recording | Indicating | Operating | Organizing | Recommending | Producing |
| Repeating | | Painting | Outlining | Reflecting | Programming |

| Remembering | Understanding | Applying | Analyzing | Evaluating | Creating |
|---|---|---|---|---|---|
| Retelling | Inferring | Playing | Planning | Reframing | Publishing |
| Retrieving | Interpreting | Preparing | Pointing out | Reviewing | Role playing |
| Searching | Journaling | Presenting | Prioritizing | Revising | Simulating |
| Selecting | Paraphrasing | Running | Questioning | Scoring | Solving |
| Tabulating | Predicting | Sharing | Separating | Supporting | Structuring |
| Telling | Relating | Sketching | Structuring | Testing | Video blogging |
| Visualizing | Subscribing | Uploading | Surveying | Validating | Wiki building |
| | Summarizing | Using | | | Writing |
| | Tagging | | | | |
| | Tweeting | | | | |

*Source: Global Digital Citizen Foundation, 2015a.*

Figure 2.3 offers definitions for the command terms we use in the sample rubric in figure 2.2 (page 29). We provide a more complete list of command terms in the appendix (page 143).

| | 1 | 2 | 3 | 4 |
|---|---|---|---|---|
| **Description** | The work states a concept. | The work outlines a concept. | The work describes a concept. | The work explains a concept. |
| **Command Term** | States: Gives a specific name, value, or other brief answer without explanation or calculation | Outlines: Gives a brief account or summary | Describes: Gives a detailed account | Explains: Gives a detailed account including causes, reasons, or mechanisms |

**Figure 2.3: Rubric including command term definitions.**

## Evidence Statements

In a fair and transparent assessment, the students should see not only the rubric teachers measure their work against but also the expectations of evidence that have contributed to their assessment, be it diagnostic, formative, or summative. If we refer back to figure 2.3, composed of a simple series of criteria, we can now add the evidence we would expect to see to attain the various phases with the following simple criteria (figure 2.4, page 32). The simple criteria for evidence are presented here as examples to help you understand the process; note that definitions can differ based on a discipline, context, or other factors, and evidence will differ as well based on the task students are to perform. It is essential that the rubric and the evidence of learning be developed at the same time and in advance of the task.

| | **1** | **2** | **3** | **4** |
|---|---|---|---|---|
| **Description** | The work states a concept. | The work outlines a concept. | The work describes a concept. | The work explains a concept. |
| **Command Term** | States: Gives a specific name, value, or other brief answer without explanation or calculation | Outlines: Gives a brief account or summary | Describes: Gives a detailed account | Explains: Gives a detailed account including causes, reasons, or mechanisms |
| **Evidence** | States the *what* | Outlines the *what* with either who, where, or when | Describes the what, where, when, and who | Explains what, where, when, who, why, and how |

**Figure 2.4: Rubric including command term definitions and evidence.**

In a completed assessment, teachers have a series of criteria that provide judgment of learning and supporting evidence statements that link the specific learning task to the criteria. In related assessments for additional tasks examining the same criteria, the rubric remains constant, but the evidence will change to reflect the new tasks. Additionally, the inclusion of evidence statements allows for transparent assessment and, when combined with completed student work, can be moderated quite well. In fact, we recommend that other faculty moderate a portion of these assessment tasks to encourage professional dialogue and ensure consistency. If the rubric and evidence are developed well, anyone doing the marking should come to a similar conclusion. This would include parents or students challenging an evaluation. When presented with the rubric, evidence statements, and the student work, it should be very clear why the work merits a designation at a certain level.

Let's look at this again as a complete process in an example from a technology class in which the teacher uses an iPod as a prompt and challenges the students to evaluate its purpose and operation. The teacher provides a rubric with the descriptions and command terms to the students at the beginning of this activity. This is essential for authentic mindful assessment. However, the teacher does not include the evidence information in the version of the rubric supplied to the class. This information is used as the marking scheme and is available to the person completing the evaluation, be it a teacher, a peer, or the students themselves. Note that when students are conducting the evaluations, the evidence statements are only supplied at the time of the evaluation—not in advance. Figure 2.5 is a rubric containing all these elements.

## *Exemplars of Student Work*

Continuing with the iPod task example, the following exemplars of student work for each phase of the rubric illustrate for teachers what student performance at each level might look like. (For context, this is an information fluency task. Any element

| | **1** | **2** | **3** | **4** |
|---|---|---|---|---|
| **Description** | The work describes the operation and purpose of the iPod. | The work explains the operation and purpose of the iPod. | The work analyzes the operation and purpose of the iPod. | The work evaluates the operation and purpose of the iPod. |
| **Command Term** | Describe: Gives a detailed account | Explain: Gives a detailed account including causes, reasons, or mechanisms | Analyze: Breaks down in order to bring out the essential elements or structure | Evaluate: Makes an appraisal by weighing up the strengths and limitations |
| **Evidence** | An account that describes what the iPod is, who made it, and possibly when or where it was manufactured or released | Evidence listed for phase one, plus how music is synchronized to the device and why this method is used | Evidence listed for phase two, with details of synchronization and operation of the device, including reference to cloud-based functions | Evidence listed for the previous phases, with detailed reference to the significance, importance, or impact of this device |

**Figure 2.5: Sample rubric including descriptions, command terms, and evidence.**

from the information fluency assessment rubrics in chapter 4 could also be added to this assessment elevating this simple task to cultivate information fluency's analytical-thinking skills—providing corollary evidence statements are developed and the original task is modified to include these requirements.) For now, we will focus just on the command terms *describe, explain, analyze,* and *evaluate* to help you to understand the evidence more clearly.

- **Phase 1:** The object is a portable music player produced by Apple called iPod. The device plays music and videos.

- **Phase 2:** The object is a portable music player produced by Apple called iPod. The device plays music and videos. Media are loaded onto the device in a variety of formats, which can include the popular MP3 format for music. The iPod is usually linked to a computer that is used to manage the content on the device.

- **Phase 3:** The object is a portable music player produced by Apple called iPod. There are different types of iPods with different features and capacities. The simplest iPod devices play music and videos. Higher-quality products allow for applications, games, Internet access, and in some cases, video conferencing. Media are loaded onto the device in a variety of formats, which can include the popular MP3 format for music. The iPod is usually linked to a computer that is used to manage the content on the device. However, in more advanced models, content may be directly downloaded onto the device via wireless connectivity.

- **Phase 4:** The object is a portable music player produced by Apple called iPod. There are different types of iPods with different features and capacities. The simplest iPod devices play music and videos. The higher-quality products such as the iPod touch allow for applications, games, Internet access, and in some cases, video conferencing.

  These features make the iPod touch a midpoint between a personal computer system and a media content device, which has the potential to lower computer, camera, and other electronic device sales, as this device contains many of these features and functions.

  Media are loaded onto the device in a variety of formats, which can include the popular MP3 format for music. The iPod is usually linked to a computer that is used to manage the content on the device. However, in more advanced models, content may be directly downloaded onto the device via wireless connectivity. This is highly effective as users will be able to connect quickly and easily to public Wi-Fi networks and access new media via application and media providers like Apple's iTunes store.

  Removing digital rights management has raised piracy issues for music and other content. Studies have shown that up to 50 percent of the average student's media is pirated. Given the popularity of this device and related devices, this raises considerable ethical and moral issues about music ownership, the related impact on the music industry, and the customers' rights. This has led to the development of streaming services such as Spotify, Rdio, and Apple Music. It is clear that the development of the iPod has irrevocably revolutionized the music industry and by extension consumer electronics.

Establishing the evidence prior to the learning activity ensures transparent, objective assessment and also makes moderation a clear process. In an attempt to be fair, many educators develop their assessment rubrics with great detail, using the evidence section as the entire rubric. However, teachers must develop both the evidence and the phase descriptions; they are two different things. The description outlines the task requirements, but the evidence dictates the marking scheme that applies to the rubric.

## Modifications for Measurement

Criterion-based assessment can also describe the level of achievement by assigning a quantity to a description. Quantity aspects are one of the most common elements we see and can be used to modify other aspects. Figure 2.6 provides an illustration of how terms that modify for quantity can be applied to distinguish different assessment phases.

Figure 2.7 provides a generic example of quantity modifications within a rubric.

| | 1 | 2 | 3 | 4 |
|---|---|---|---|---|
| **Quantity Aspect** | Few, little, slightly | Some, somewhat, partially | Most, mostly, the majority of | All or the vast majority |

**Figure 2.6: Applications of quantifying terms within a rubric.**

| | 1 | 2 | 3 | 4 |
|---|---|---|---|---|
| **Description** | The product contains a *few* of the required elements. | The product contains *some* of the required elements. | The product contains *many* of the required elements. | The product contains *all* the required elements. |

**Figure 2.7: Rubric including quantity aspect.**

Let's think about the aspect of accuracy. Accuracy is basically an absolute; something is either accurate or it isn't. However, in cases of seeming absolutes, we can apply quantifiable language to measure such items within the four levels of the rubric. See figure 2.8 for an example of the absolute language, the alternative possibilities for applying quantity, and the resulting description.

| | 1 | 2 | 3 | 4 |
|---|---|---|---|---|
| **Initial Description** | The work is unsupported. | not applicable | not applicable | The work is supported and cited. |
| **Accuracy and Detail Aspect (in absolutes)** | The work is unsupported, opinion based, inaccurate, flawed assumption | not applicable | not applicable | The work has a high degree of accuracy and attention to detail, is supported and cited, and precise. |
| **Quantity Aspect** | The work is few, little, slightly. | The work is some, somewhat, partially. | The work is most, mostly, the majority of. | The work is all or the vast majority. |
| **Final Description** | The work provides little research, and the research is not cited. | The work provides research that is partially cited. | The work provides detailed research, the majority of which is cited. | The work provides detailed research that is thoroughly cited. |

**Figure 2.8: Rubric descriptions before and after applying quantity to absolutes.**

Figure 2.9 (page 36) lists some additional aspects that are absolutes and their opposites, which a teacher could turn into a complete rubric by making modifications that apply the quantity aspect, as demonstrated in figure 2.8.

These rubrics not only help teachers identify students' achievement and needs but also allow them to understand expectations, set goals, and identify their own progress.

| | Aspect | Opposite |
|---|---|---|
| **Accuracy and Detail** | High degree of accuracy, attention to detail, supported and cited, detailed, precise | Unsupported, opinion, inaccurate, incorrect, flawed assumption |
| **Suitability and Appropriateness** | Suitable, appropriate, well matched, aligns to, applicable, correct, fitting | Unsuitable, inappropriate |
| **Flow** | Logical progress, flows, continuity | Little flow, no logical progression, discontinuous |
| **Clarity** | Clear, transparent, accurate, easily decipherable or understood | Vague, unclear, inaccurate, misleading, hidden, inexplicable |
| **Performance** | Compelling, accurate, focused, precise, persuading, captivating | Inaccurate, poorly focused, imprecise, distracting, tiresome, tedious |

**Figure 2.9: Additional rubric aspects that teachers can modify by applying quantities.**

For all the essential fluencies' elements, we have identified student achievement criteria at each phase of the assessment framework this chapter outlines, which we will provide in rubric form over the next several chapters. Note that in some instances, not all phases will be applicable to all items we identify. There are times and places where it's not possible or doesn't make sense to expect students to perform at each level (for instance, when a rubric is measuring a student's performance with recording information sources or obtaining information, the fourth phase, which involves creating, does not apply). Also, because the fluencies are interconnected and overlap at times (for example, parts of information fluency appear in the solution fluency discover aspect, but are applied differently depending on the fluency task), the same or similar items will be applicable to more than one fluency and will therefore appear in more than one rubric.

You can employ the fluencies assessment framework by using our assessment rubrics as a basis and applying the dimensions discussed in this chapter—including assessment language, evidence statements, and quantifying language—based on the tasks students will perform in the lessons and assignments you design.

# Guiding Questions

Before moving to the next chapter, answer the following questions as an individual or with your school team.

1. What are the pros and cons of the different types of learning assessment we use?

2. What are the essential elements of successful education design?

3. How can we improve our own education design?

4. Why is it important for our students to understand how and why they are being assessed?

5. What are the benefits of allowing students to self- and peer-assess?

# chapter 3

# Solution Fluency

Cultivating problem-solving skills is a top priority, a concept echoed in curricula around the world. From Australia's general capabilities to New Zealand's key competencies to the learner profile of the International Baccalaureate program to the NGA and CCSSO's Common Core, problem-solving abilities top the list of what these standards demand. Industry and schools alike repeatedly emphasize the critical need to develop this capacity in students.

In his book *The Overflowing Brain*, Torkel Klingberg (2009) states that if you teach students a structured problem-solving process to the level of unconscious application (or fluency), they will instantaneously increase their IQ by 10 percent and sustain this increase throughout their lives. So how do we develop problem-solving skills? The obvious answer is to solve problems, but the school culture is focused on instruction and not inquiry. This was our primary drive in writing *Literacy Is Not Enough* (Crockett et al., 2011): to demonstrate how to shift from teacher-centered to learner-centered instruction. We defined an innovative learning environment as one in which students use higher-order thinking to create learning products as solutions to relevant real-world problems. To do this, we employ the 6Ds of solution fluency—(1) define, (2) discover, (3) dream, (4) design, (5) deliver, and (6) debrief. In this chapter, we will describe these aspects, note some of the skills each helps to cultivate, and list potential benefits that result from developing those skills. We then provide rubrics for measuring items that students require to be successful with the aspects of solution fluency.

## Define

Learners must first clearly define what the problem is in order to solve a problem. They need context and a list of potential solutions. While this includes being able to restate the problem with accuracy and clarity, fluency requires much more. They must also be able to reflect critically and independently on the purpose and sequence, asking themselves, "What do I need to do?" This requires breaking tasks down to component elements, sequencing them logically, understanding how to apply tasks and skills to the process, and evaluating completeness. The strategies, skills, and processes that students develop in the define stage, and the beneficial opportunities and possibilities that utilizing each creates, include the following.

- Restating or rephrasing the problem:
  - Causes learners to think about the problem from different perspectives, leading to more versatile solutions
  - Reveals things about the problem that may not be obvious
  - Can lead to creating solutions for multiple problems
  - Leads to hearing unique perspectives from others
- Challenging assumptions:
  - Helps learners understand how the problem may have originated
  - Challenges learners to consider an issue in different ways
  - Helps learners question assumptions that limit independent thought
  - Teaches learners to decide for themselves what is right and true
- Researching and gathering facts:
  - Provides opportunities for developing useful research and data analysis
  - Allows learners to discover surprising things about a problem they didn't know before
  - Helps learners avoid making assumptions and forming opinions without ample information
  - Gives learners time to think about why finding a solution to the problem is important

# Discover

If the define question asks "What do I need to do?" the discover question asks "What do I need to know and be able to do?" Learners must decide exactly what they need to solve and give proper context to the problem.

Discover is connected intrinsically to information fluency, which we will discuss in more depth in the next chapter. Discover addresses the surface levels of what information fluency explores extensively. It requires developing a series of probing and inquiring questions, as well as accessing a range of suitable and authoritative primary and secondary information sources. Further, students must evaluate each information source's validity, and support the most critical information sources with multiple sources. The strategies, skills, and processes that students develop in the discover stage, and the beneficial opportunities and possibilities that utilizing each creates, include the following.

- Locating information:
  - Teaches effective search skills
  - Creates awareness that various sources are not complete, or not a one-stop shop for all learners' information needs
  - Develops habits of mind for asking the best possible questions
  - Teaches learners to be inquisitive and analytical about what they're trying to solve
- Skimming, scanning, and scouring data for background:
  - Cultivates the ability to determine at a glance what might be useful
  - Develops organizational skills
  - Improves future information quests with practice of these techniques
- Filtering:
  - Teaches learners to identify facts and how they can convey them to inform or shape the audience's opinion
  - Cultivates the ability to differentiate fact from opinion
- Taking smart notes:
  - Trains learners to be better listeners
  - Develops better information organization skills
  - Encourages learners not to be mechanical writers but rather to consider the real goal for taking notes on a subject
  - Helps students learn to be brief and concise and focus on what's important
- Analyzing, authenticating, and arranging materials:
  - Cultivates critical thinking
  - Teaches learners to be analytical—not cynical—about what information is offered
  - Encourages the habit of checking information sources for validity and currency, an important practice in information gathering

# Dream

In the dream stage, learners open their hearts and minds to possibilities and visions of a solution. In other words, "What do I want it to look like?" This solution fluency phase is about imagination, extrapolation, and visualization. One of the greatest challenges in the dream stage is to truly embrace the possibilities. Too quickly students can limit themselves through negative self-talk. This can arise in the form of self-doubt, or more commonly in their resistance to change by focusing not on the possibilities, but on all the reasons why they can't do it. In our experience, primary school students are much less resistant to this process than adults. Students quickly come up with dozens of unique and imaginative solutions, though not all of them are practical or achievable. This is why it is so critical to develop problem-solving skills at an early age. Students demonstrating what they can do is empowering for them! The strategies, skills, and processes that students develop in the dream stage, and the beneficial opportunities and possibilities that utilizing each creates, include the following.

- Generating wishes:
  - Allows learners to break all bonds of their thinking and envision a perfect solution from which to work backward
  - Encourages learners to be fearless in brainstorming and sharing their ideas
  - Inspires learners and invokes a stronger drive toward finding solutions
- Exploring possibilities:
  - Guides learners toward challenging assumptions and beliefs that hold them back
  - Teaches learners to be brave and courageous with their vision
  - Teaches learners to keep a positive frame of mind when solving problems
  - Helps learners discover that the impossible may sometimes be possible
- Imagining best-case scenarios:
  - Helps learners remain inspired to develop the best possible solution
  - Encourages brainstorming activities that hone communication skills
  - Lets learners be free with their ideas, and develops positive and constructive mindsets from team members
  - Guides learners toward thinking in terms of possibilities and helps them transcend limited thinking
- Visualizing what they would consider a perfect future:
  - Helps learners continue to explore positive possibilities
  - Provides an effective visualization exercise in which learners can be clear about how they want their solution's outcome to look in real life
  - Helps learners envision a better world for present and future generations

# Design

In the design phase, students begin using gathered knowledge to synthesize solutions. They create goals and milestones, assign team roles, and create accountability systems for the whole team. Often people confuse the design phase with the design of a finished product, which is really something that occurs in the dream stage. Design is about designing the process that learners will implement to arrive at the envisioned solution, or asking "How am I going to get there?"

Starting with a future point in mind and working backward is how this process is built. There are many reasons for this. The present (define) focuses on the problem and the way things are at the moment, but focusing on the envisioned solution (dream) is a much more powerful mindset. With a firm vision of the successful future outcome, begin by asking, "What happened before this?" For example, if the future vision involves a movie presented to an enthusiastic audience, don't start from the beginning, but from the outcome, the successful presentation of the movie, and ask "What happened before this?" Perhaps it was film editing, and what happened before the editing was the filming, and what happened before the filming was the writing, and so on. These become the major milestones in the plan. Next, consider the interim steps. This is how one builds a project plan or design, which takes students from where they are to where they want to be. When standing in the present, and looking toward the future, it can be difficult to consider what to do to get there. Even the first step can be excruciating and can cause paralysis in the process for fear of not succeeding or of going in the wrong direction. The potential roadblocks can seem overwhelming. But if we think about the dream as if it is a reality, asking the question of what happened before is simple. The walk backwards from the future while looking forward creates a perfect plan as it also naturally sidesteps all roadblocks. The strategies, skills, and processes that students develop in the design stage, and the beneficial opportunities and possibilities that utilizing each creates, include the following.

- Focusing on the future:
  - Keeps everyone aligned toward the end goal
  - Makes sure everyone looks out for each other in order to foster the collaborative spirit
  - Offers a chance for team members to share initial opinions, concerns, and suggestions before the project development begins
- Starting at the end and building backward:
  - Creates a habit of logical, organized thinking
  - Inspires confidence in team members to achieve the goal
  - Eliminates the dangers and uncertainties of *flying blind* (completing an assignment without knowing its expectations or what students are supposed to learn)
  - Introduces structure and a clear strategy for progression in problem solving and project management

- Creating instructions:

  - Establishes a good communication practice for explaining a task's logical steps

  - Helps learners consider others' viewpoints as they create a set of instructions that everyone can broadly understand

  - Develops logical thinking patterns

# Deliver

Designing a presentation isn't enough; it has to be presented. Writing a song isn't enough; it has to be recorded. Developing a script isn't enough; the work has to be performed. Students must, in essence, *deliver* the goods. Without fully implementing a solution, they have not solved the original problem and they do not know if their solution will work. That's where the deliver stage comes in. It's where we ask ourselves, How do I make it happen? or How am I going to get there? The deliver phase happens in two separate stages—(1) produce and (2) publish. It involves both completing the solution (produce) and then making the actual presentation or demonstration (publish). The strategies, skills, and processes that students develop in the deliver stage, and the beneficial opportunities and possibilities that utilizing each creates, include the following.

- Identifying the appropriate format for presentation:

  - Uses the best visual solutions, which is critical for success in many modern fields of employment and education alike

  - Helps students learn about how new technologies work and how they can be used in classroom projects

  - Teaches learners to focus on the message and how it shapes people's thinking instead of just passively consuming what they see

  - Guides learners toward considering what they really want to accomplish with any message they share

  - Lets learners consider the delivery more carefully and critically

  - Encourages learners to get to know about their audience beforehand so they develop interest in others

- Demonstrating or presenting the solution:

  - Lets learners test the solution by applying it against the challenge

  - Gives learners a chance to revisit other solution fluency stages to refine and improve the solution

  - Raises questions from both learners and the audience about what works and what they could improve

- Teaches learners to respect and consider others' opinions
- Cultivates confidence and how to share opinions in a constructive manner

# Debrief

During the debrief stage, students look at their projects from beginning to end and really get to own their learning. They determine what they could have done better and ways they could improve their problem-solving approach in similar situations. The problem becomes personal when learners take ownership of it. The solution is also deeply personal for students as it is their own creation. Because of this, they have a strong sense of accountability. This is where we consider the questions, "What were my results, and what did I learn from them? How could I make this product and the process better?" In our experience, once students have been involved in the debrief phase, they start to prepare by themselves and make improvements to their products before they present them. The strategies, skills, and processes that students develop in the debrief stage, and the beneficial opportunities and possibilities that utilizing each creates, include the following.

- Revisiting and reflecting on the product or process:
  - Sets the tone for a lengthier discussion about how students used the 6Ds to create the solution to the challenge
  - Teaches learners more about big-picture thinking and broader perspectives
  - Develops collaborative communication skills
- Asking good questions about the product or process:
  - Reveals what students can improve on when addressing similar problems in the future
  - Teaches learners to improve processes to make them more versatile
  - Continues the collaborative skill development when working in teams
  - Allows learners to recognize each team member's specific contributions
- Internalizing and using new learning:
  - Makes the learning stick—the more learners practice this process, the more fluent they become
  - Makes problem solving easier with an internalized process like the 6Ds
  - Allows learners to see problems as opportunities for greater learning
  - Better prepares learners to handle future challenges

# Solution Fluency in Schools

Since first introducing solution fluency in 2011, we have found the pace at which solution fluency has been implemented in schools around the world to be staggering. Schools looking for guidance in fine-tuning the process constantly contact us. We have been incredibly inspired by what we have seen.

The aforementioned Wilderness School, a girls' school in Adelaide, Australia, was the first school in the country to partner with us in adopting the fluencies, recognizing that these fluencies are processes that mirror the general capabilities outlined in the Australian Curriculum (visit www.australiancurriculum.edu.au for more about these standards). Wilderness remains a top school because of its culture of excellence—understanding that excellence is a moving target and that constant innovation is essential maintenance. Solution fluency has been used with Wilderness students of all ages—from three-year-olds in the early learning center through senior students—with tremendous results and outstanding student products. More importantly, it's not just being used for school—the administration and students have transferred it over into the real world and transformed how they work.

The administration uses solution fluency as its primary process in strategic planning, through which it has seen significant productivity gains as the streamlined process of solution fluency is commonly understood and practiced. Senior students have been using solution fluency to create a legacy project. The challenge they defined for themselves is to "enhance the culture of Wilderness by ensuring every girl feels connected, respected and heard" (Dinh, 2015, p. 2). They have developed an extensive set of criteria of what this means and how it can be measured, and a very thorough plan for making it a reality.

A shining moment for us at a visit to Wilderness was when four-year-old students in the early learning center explained to their parents the 6Ds of the solution fluency process and showed them how they have been using them. To see students at this age able to utilize a structured problem-solving process so thoroughly is awe inspiring. The challenge Wilderness now faces is how the junior and senior schools will have to change to accommodate these students. What a wonderful problem to have!

Following are exemplars of inquiry- and project-based lessons that cultivate solution fluency. We've provided samples that cover a variety of grade levels and subjects to ensure all readers have access to relevant, applicable examples. Readers can find the full lessons as well as the activities and assessment resources on the Solution Fluency Activity Planner (https://solutionfluency.com). See the extensive rubrics at the end of this chapter (figures 3.1–3.6, pages 47–54) for tools to facilitate assessment of these and other solution fluency lessons.

## Brainy Inventions (Primary School)

**Essential question:** How can knowledge of the local and global market improve an invention, gadget, or tool?

**Subjects:** Mathematics, history, arts, science, language arts, design

**Scenario:** What happens when an invention or gadget is no longer as useful to people and its sales are down? Give it an update—use solution fluency to breathe new life into an old idea! Your group of inventors will add an improvement or redesign to an obsolete invention or gadget to make it work better and once again become useful to people. Use creative designs, storytelling, mathematics, and science to work with your team to make something that's old relevant again!

## Hidden Treasure (Primary School)

**Essential question:** How can your knowledge of science and geography help with making decisions when searching for precious gems and metals?

**Subjects:** Geography, science, language arts, technology

**Scenario:** Have you ever imagined what it would be like to hunt for hidden treasure? A local mine is struggling to find new deposits—and if no new mineral deposits are found soon, the mine will face closure, and many people in your area will lose their jobs. Imagine you and your school friends have decided to help by creating a treasure map that shows possible locations where such precious metals and gemstones could be found. Present your map with at least five locations for mineral deposits, and give descriptions of how these minerals are formed. Rock on!

## Photo Power (Middle School)

**Essential question:** How does littering affect our health and the environment?

**Subjects:** Language arts, science, social studies, design, environmental studies

**Scenario:** A local chapter of a large environmentalist group has approached your advertising team. They want you to create a poster and e-brochure designed to bring awareness to the problem of litter in your community. In your designs, use powerful images and write action statements for each one. Provide statistics that define littering as a growing problem and its environmental effects, and suggestions for what can be done to address the concern. Inspire people to work together in cleaning up your community!

## Design Star (Middle School)

**Essential question:** How can interior designers use mathematics to bring their visions to life?

**Subjects:** Mathematics, language arts, design, art, technology

**Scenario:** A successful designer is one who has an innate sense of style and a solid mathematical foundation. Could you succeed in the design industry? This is a great way to find out! Select a messy or uninspiring space to redesign, and build a scale model to display your vision. Plan the new design and build a diorama that displays the space's major lengths, widths, and heights to scale. Then put your design mojo to work! You can create a video or slideshow that captures the design process along with before shots of the chosen space and after shots of your scale model. Design your perfect space!

## Off to Space (High School)

**Essential question:** How can we use our knowledge of mathematics to help with space travel?

**Subjects:** Mathematics, science, language arts, astronomy, media, technology

**Scenario:** Could space tourism ever become a reality? You certainly think so! Why not share your idea using the creative impact of digital media in designing an itinerary for an interstellar guided tour? Create a three-minute video outlining a proposed itinerary for a guided space tour, including some interesting information about each place you will visit along the way. The numbers representing distances and other quantities involved in intergalactic space travel can be very large, so use both decimal and scientific notations in your video. Take the ultimate trip through the cosmos!

## Feeding the Need (High School)

**Essential question:** How does proper nutrition help sufferers of chronic illnesses?

**Subjects:** Science, language arts, mathematics, nutrition, technology

**Scenario:** When the body is healthy, the mind is healthy, and everything just feels good. But sometimes our systems become unbalanced due to chronic illnesses, and we turn to the healing power of food to restore the balance within us. Nobody knows about that more than you, so show your food smarts! Develop a publication that features an interesting visual reference for food sources containing vitamins the human body needs. Include food sources that can help those suffering from a low level of vitamins C, D, B, and others. Create a one-stop guide for becoming a nutritional powerhouse!

# Rubrics for Solution Fluency

We provide the following rubrics as examples for evaluating student performance on items that contribute to solution fluency, including descriptions of what student performance or work products might look like at each phase of the essential fluencies framework.

| **Define** | **Phase 1**<br>(awareness, connection, remembering) | **Phase 2**<br>(understanding, applying) | **Phase 3**<br>(analyzing, evaluating) | **Phase 4**<br>(evaluating, creating) |
|---|---|---|---|---|
| Understanding of task purpose | • Develops a definition of the problem that is a repeat of the stimulus material | • Develops a definition of the problem that shows an understanding of the tasks and how skills will be applied to the process | • Develops a definition of the problem by removing extraneous information<br>• Breaks the task or definition down into components<br>• Sequences components in a logical progression | • Develops a definition of the problem that shows critical reflection on the task<br>• Breaks the task or definition down into components<br>• Sequences components in a logical progression<br>• Evaluates the definition for completeness |
| Independence | • Shows little independence<br>• Requires extensive support to develop or adapt the definition | • Demonstrates some independence<br>• Seeks teacher or peer feedback to successfully develop or adapt the definition | • Shows ability to break the task into elements and then work through them with a degree of independence and self-management<br>• Analyzes feedback to consider its merit, using it if appropriate<br>• Requires little input from the teacher to successfully develop or adapt the definition | • Demonstrates an ability to be self-critical, monitoring his or her own progress and reflecting on it<br>• Shows ability to modify his or her planning and schedule as a result<br>• Requires little or no input from the teacher to successfully develop or adapt the definition |
| Accuracy and clarity | • Develops a basic definition that would enable a solution | • Develops a definition that would enable the production of a successful solution and sets some of the success criteria | • Develops a definition that would enable the production of a successful solution, is broken down into its component parts, and includes most of the success criteria for the solution | • Develops a definition that would enable the production of a successful solution, is clear and concise, has been (where required) revised to remove extraneous information, and includes detailed success criteria for the solution |
| Critical reflection | • Does not revisit or revise the definition during the solution fluency process | • Adapts the assigned task during the solution fluency process | • Breaks down the task definition into the components and identifies the relationship between each<br>• Updates the analysis as further information comes to hand | • Critically reviews and adapts the task definition (if required) while progressing through the solution fluency process |

*Visit **go.SolutionTree.com/assessment** for a free reproducible version of this figure.*

**Figure 3.1: Solution fluency assessment rubric—Define.**

| Discover | Phase 1 (awareness, connection, remembering) | Phase 2 (understanding, applying) | Phase 3 (analyzing, evaluating) | Phase 4 (evaluating, creating) |
|---|---|---|---|---|
| **Develops questions** | • Identifies some key words and states basic questions to collect some pertinent information for the task based on the definition; some questions and key words are redundant or irrelevant; many questions are closed | • Identifies a suitable range of relevant key words and uses these to develop some probing and inquiring questions; most questions are task-focused and will yield useful information; there are few closed questions | • Breaks the problem down into its components and identifies a suitable range of relevant key words; these are used to develop a range of inquiry questions that are focused on the problem; the questions enable effective and efficient access to information | • Identifies a suitable range of relevant key words and uses these to develop a range of inquiry questions that are focused on the definition and that enable effective and efficient access to a broad and suitable range of information sources<br>• Reflects on and refines the questions as required |
| **Accesses suitable information sources** | • Accesses the provided resources | • Accesses a range of resources, including and beyond provided options, most of which are suitable and authoritative | • Accesses a range of select suitable and authoritative resources, which could include appropriate primary sources | • Creatively accesses a broad range of suitable and imaginative resources, which could include primary sources |
| **Validates information** | • Does not validate information for accuracy or factual basis | • Applies basic techniques for validating information sources | • Applies a variety of suitable techniques to critically evaluate each information source's validity<br>• Provides multiple information sources to support critical information<br>• Can break down information into component parts and compare different elements' validity | • Applies a variety of suitable techniques to critically evaluate each information source's validity<br>• Provides multiple information sources to support critical information<br>• Can break down information into component parts and evaluate different elements' validity<br>• Can justify the process undertaken and information's validity |

| <br>**Discover** | **Phase 1**<br>(awareness, connection, remembering) | **Phase 2**<br>(understanding, applying) | **Phase 3**<br>(analyzing, evaluating) | **Phase 4**<br>(evaluating, creating) |
|---|---|---|---|---|
| **Applies information** | • Makes some use of the collected information; much of the information is in its original form; there is little refinement of the information | • Applies the collected information to develop a broad understanding of the task, its background, and so on<br>• Sometimes recognizes areas of limited information or validity and refines searches or instigates new ones | • Uses the collected and collated information to structure the task<br>• Reviews the information and makes critical judgments on the depth and breadth of knowledge the task requires<br>• Recognizes areas of limited information or validity and refines searches or undertakes new searches to correct them<br>• Includes some evaluation of the information's validation and accuracy | • Creatively uses the processed information to structure the task<br>• Critically reviews the information and makes critical judgments on the depth and breadth of information the task requires<br>• Applies information from multiple differing sources and media using imaginative and focused strategies and techniques<br>• Recognizes areas of limited information or validity and refines or undertakes new searches to correct them<br>• Includes evaluation of the information's validity and accuracy |
| **Records and acknowledges information sources** | • Recalls a simple list of resources used with little or no formatting or processing | • Applies suitable citation techniques to develop an appropriate bibliography | • Consistently and accurately uses suitable methods to provide a detailed and structured bibliography of information sources; sources are suitably organized and presented; primary information sources are suitably acknowledged, and permission is sought to use resources where appropriate | • not applicable |

*Visit **go.SolutionTree.com/assessment** for a free reproducible version of this figure.*

**Figure 3.2: Solution fluency assessment rubric—Discover.**

| Dream | Phase 1 (awareness, connection, remembering) | Phase 2 (understanding, applying) | Phase 3 (analyzing, evaluating) | Phase 4 (evaluating, creating) |
|---|---|---|---|---|
| **Identifies the audience and considers their needs, preferences, and motivations** | • Identifies the outcome and the audience | • Identifies and states the audience<br>• Outlines some of the requirements of the audience | • Is able to evaluate most of the audience's needs and relate them to the task | • Is able to evaluate, in depth, the audience's needs and relate them to the task or outcome in detail |
| **Creatively combines elements of different stimuli and sources, personal experiences, and underlying principles of the medium to a unique creative outcome** | • Views different sources that might apply to the task and definition | • Considers a limited range of sources and some of the underlying rules of the medium as they apply to the task and definition | • Considers different stimuli and sources, his or her own personal experiences, and some of the underlying rules of the medium as they apply to the task and definition | • Creatively and imaginatively considers different stimuli and sources, his or her own personal experiences and preferences, and the underlying rules of the medium or elements of the material as they apply to the task and definition |
| **Presents a range of solutions (when possible) and considers the most appropriate and achievable one** | • Proposes a single solution, which will address some of the components of the problem<br>• Struggles to consider the solution's viability or feasibility | • Proposes a solution or a limited number of solutions that would address the majority of the components of the problem<br>• Applies some criteria to select the solution | • Proposes a range of solutions that will solve the problem<br>• Identifies the different components of the problem for each solution<br>• Selects the solution based on the success criteria<br>• Provides some justification of the selection | • Proposes a range of creative and imaginative solutions that will solve the problem; the proposed solutions are linked to stimulus material and resources he or she has discovered; there is critical reflection on the positives and negatives of each solution<br>• Uses the success criteria to select the most feasible solution for further development<br>• Justifies his or her decision clearly |
| **Communicates solution, decision, and selection process effectively** | • Can outline his or her decision and selection process | • Can describe or explain his or her solution to the problem, decisions, and selection process | • Can analyze his or her solution to the problem, decisions, and selection process | • Can fluently and articulately justify his or her selection, judgment, critique, decisions, and processes |

*Visit* **go.SolutionTree.com/assessment** *for a free reproducible version of this figure.*

**Figure 3.3: Solution fluency assessment rubric—Dream.**

| ![Design] Design | Phase 1 (awareness, connection, remembering) | Phase 2 (understanding, applying) | Phase 3 (analyzing, evaluating) | Phase 4 (evaluating, creating) |
|---|---|---|---|---|
| **Develops a complete plan, schematic, or similar design concept for the solution** | • Develops a plan that would create some of the aspects of the product successfully; a number of areas of development are incomplete or outlined only briefly; the plan contains insufficient details to allow for a clear understanding of the process | • Develops a plan that will lead to the development of a product or solution; most of the areas of development of the product are covered; the plan contains details that would allow the product to be created, but a third party would struggle to understand the process clearly | • Breaks down the overall plan into suitable components<br>• Analyzes the plan to ensure all elements are accounted for<br>• Evaluates and modifies the plan, time line, or design to ensure that the product will be produced | • Develops a creative design to produce the product<br>• Uses the rules of the medium to develop the completed design; the design is complete and has suitable detail in all of the component parts; the plan is analyzed and broken down into suitable parts; the plan, process, and product are evaluated against the definition and the envisioned solution; changes are justifiable |
| **Breaks down the process into suitable phases, tasks, or steps** | • Produces a list of stages or steps | • Produces a logical list of stages or steps<br>• Provides some detail for each stage or step; the plan is clear enough that a third party could understand the process being planned or undertaken | • Analyzes the product and breaks the task into suitable stages<br>• Suitably details and considers each stage; stages are logically sequenced<br>• Sufficiently details and structures the plan so that a third party could easily understand the process | • Analyzes the product and breaks the task into suitable stages<br>• Suitably details and considers each stage; stages are logically sequenced<br>• Evaluates the efficiency of the process and modifies dynamically as required<br>• Sufficiently details and structures the plan so that a third party could easily understand the process |
| **Assigns time for each stage** | • Assigns a time to each stage with little consideration of the complexity of the stage or step | • Assigns a time to each stage with consideration of the complexity of the stage or step; much of the timing is realistic | • Produces a realistic estimation<br>• Evaluates time assigned to each stage<br>• Adjusts and modifies process as required<br>• Informs stakeholders of significant changes with some evaluation of reasons for changes | • Produces a realistic and mostly accurate estimation<br>• Has considered a wide range of factors in the development of the timing for the stages and has included contingency and flexibility<br>• Critically evaluates time assigned to each stage<br>• Can apply suitable planning and management models to provide structure<br>• Adjusts and modifies process as required<br>• Informs stakeholders of significant changes with detailed evaluation of reasons for changes |

**Figure 3.4: Solution fluency assessment rubric—Design.** continued →

| Design | Phase 1 (awareness, connection, remembering) | Phase 2 (understanding, applying) | Phase 3 (analyzing, evaluating) | Phase 4 (evaluating, creating) |
|---|---|---|---|---|
| **Assigns responsibility for aspects of the development as required** | • Assigns each team member a role | • Assigns roles to team members<br>• Has considered some of the limiting factors and abilities of the team when assigning roles<br>• Checks on progress and updates the schedule | • Analyzes the tasks and assigns roles<br>• Balances the workload with some consideration of team members' strengths and abilities<br>• Considers most limiting factors<br>• Frequently checks on progress and updates the schedule | • Analyzes the tasks and evaluates all team members' strengths<br>• Assigns tasks based on team members' suitability, availability, and skill sets<br>• Considers limiting factors<br>• Frequently analyzes process and evaluates deadlines and task objectives, adjusting them as required |
| **Considers feasibility of the solution** | • Selects a product with minimal consideration for feasibility or suitability | • Briefly considers some of the factors of feasibility and suitability before accepting or rejecting the solution | • Considers the feasibility of the solution by breaking down the feasibility into component parts including time, skills, cost, availability of materials, hardware, and software<br>• Considers the purpose of the product and the requirements of the target audience<br>• Checks the solution against the success criteria before accepting or rejecting the product or solution | • Evaluates the feasibility of the solution as criteria for selecting the product design<br>• Considers a range of factors including time, skills, cost, availability of materials, hardware, and software<br>• Considers the purpose of the product and the requirements of the target audience<br>• Where necessary, considers marketability, appropriateness, and sustainability<br>• Checks the solution against the success criteria<br>• Modifies the solution or selects a new solution if the product is not feasible |

*Visit **go.SolutionTree.com/assessment** for a free reproducible version of this figure.*

| ![rocket] Deliver | Phase 1 (awareness, connection, remembering) | Phase 2 (understanding, applying) | Phase 3 (analyzing, evaluating) | Phase 4 (evaluating, creating) |
|---|---|---|---|---|
| Revisits, reflects critically on, and revises the process at each stage and maintains a focus on the goals driving the problem-solving process | • Refers to the plan periodically<br>• Can state the stage of the plan he or she is in<br>• Needs support to remain on task and focused | • Monitors his or her progress against the plan<br>• Offers some reflection on how the process or product is being undertaken<br>• Identifies aspects needing revision and applies changes<br>• Has a suitable level of focus of the outcome and goals of the process | • Monitors and evaluates progress<br>• Offers some reflection on the process or product and how this could be improved<br>• Identifies aspects needing revision and applies changes<br>• Is partly able to justify modifications and decisions<br>• Maintains a focus on the goals and outcomes | • Evaluates his or her progress and critically reflects on the process and product and how they could be improved<br>• Makes suitable modifications to the process and can provide detailed justifications of these<br>• Maintains a consistent focus on the overall goals and outcomes, considering these critically when adapting and modifying |
| Produces the product consistently with the design | • Develops a product or outcome that is partially functional or complete, addresses some of the success criteria, and is partly suitable for the audience or purpose | • Develops a product that is mostly consistent with the design, meets some of the success criteria, and is functional | • Develops a product that is suitable for the purpose and audience, is consistent with the design, meets most of the success criteria, and is functional<br>• Identifies changes from the original plan, process, or design and can justify some of them | • Develops a product that is suitable for the purpose and audience, is consistent with the design, meets the success criteria, is fully functional, and shows care and attention to detail<br>• Fully justifies any changes from the original plan, process, or design |
| Produces the product within the constraints and success criteria set in the design stage | • Struggles to remain within the process constraints<br>• Has some awareness of the limitations, restrictions, and so on | • Applies the criteria and generally remains within the process constraints<br>• Is able to state the process and product's goals, outcomes, and limitations | • Consistently analyzes and breaks down the process and product and compares against the success criteria<br>• Offers some limited evaluation and sometimes revises the design, success criteria, and plan<br>• Can partly justify changes and modifications | • Consistently analyzes and evaluates the process and product against the success criteria to ensure accuracy<br>• Evaluates and revises the design, success criteria, and plan as required<br>• Is able to justify the changes and modifications as required<br>• Informs stakeholders of substantial changes if required |
| Works efficiently | • Sometimes is accurate in his or her execution of the plan or product development | • Can apply the plan or design with some accuracy; there is some waste in terms of time, effort, and materials or resources | • Generally works efficiently with minimal waste in terms of time, effort, and materials or resources<br>• Demonstrates general accuracy in the execution of his or her plan, product development, and his or her reflection | • Works with efficiency in a manner that is economical in terms of time, effort, and materials or resources<br>• Works with accuracy in the execution of his or her plan, product development, and reflection |

*Visit* **go.SolutionTree.com/assessment** *for a free reproducible version of this figure.*

**Figure 3.5: Solution fluency assessment rubric—Deliver.**

| Debrief | Phase 1 (awareness, connection, remembering) | Phase 2 (understanding, applying) | Phase 3 (analyzing, evaluating) | Phase 4 (evaluating, creating) |
|---|---|---|---|---|
| **Demonstrates adaptability and commitment by modifying the product and the process when weaknesses in either are identified** | • Struggles to remain on task and within the constraints for the process | • Applies the criteria and generally remains within the constraints of the process, with little or no deviation from, or modification of, the original plan or design | • Analyzes and breaks down the process and product<br>• Compares progress against the success criteria and plan<br>• Sometimes revises design, success criteria, and plan<br>• Offers some limited evaluation and partly justifies changes and modifications | • Consistently analyzes and evaluates the process and product against the success criteria, plan, and process to ensure accuracy<br>• Evaluates and revises the success criteria, plan, design, or product as required<br>• Justifies the changes and modifications |
| **Reflects critically on how to improve the product and process once a solution is developed** | • Provides reflection that is often superficial and incomplete<br>• May offer some next steps, but these are not linked to the reflection | • Provides some reflection on the different stages of the process undertaken; reflection is generally fair and appropriate<br>• Proposes some valid next steps | • Provides a suitable analysis (stage by stage) and some evaluation of the process undertaken; reflection is fair, thoughtful, deliberate, and appropriate overall<br>• Provides some next steps based on the evaluation | • Provides a clear and concise evaluation of the process undertaken; reflection is fair, thoughtful, deliberate, and appropriate<br>• Provides a detailed reflection, and then develops clear next steps in consideration of this (where required) |

*Visit* **go.SolutionTree.com/assessment** *for a free reproducible version of this figure.*

**Figure 3.6: Solution fluency assessment rubric—Debrief.**

We often refer to solution fluency as the baseline fluency because many parts of the other fluencies are contained within it. As students gain more confidence with solution fluency, we can begin to peel back each phase, like layers of an onion, to show the deeper levels, which we will see in the subsequent fluencies discussed in the remaining chapters.

# Guiding Questions

Before moving to the next chapter, answer the following questions as an individual or with your school team.

1. Considering what you now know, what do you feel are the defining characteristics of an exceptional problem solver?

2. What are the reasons why developing independent problem-solving skills in students is being given such heavy focus globally in modern education?

3. What are the questions in each stage of the 6Ds that define the stage's essential meaning, and how can they help you and your students understand the solution fluency process?

4. In what situations and environments, other than educational ones, do you feel solution fluency can be applied in our daily lives?

5. The fluencies are not linear processes, but rather cyclical processes. What does this mean, and how can it benefit those using these processes in learning?

# chapter 4

# Information Fluency

We live in an age of disposable information. While it retains value, it is simply more perishable now due to its sheer volume and ever-changing nature. Every day, we create 2.5 quintillion bytes of data—so much that 90 percent of the data in the world today was created in the last two years alone (IBM, n.d.)! With so much transforming and multiplying data surrounding us, it's increasingly difficult to claim absolute expertise on anything.

We must teach our students to be fluent with information. Thus, we present information fluency as the ability to mechanically and intuitively interpret information in all forms and formats in order to extract the essential knowledge, perceive its meaning and significance, and use it to complete real-world tasks. The information fluency process has five distinct aspects: (1) ask, (2) acquire, (3) analyze, (4) apply, and (5) assess. In this chapter, we will describe these aspects, note some of the skills each helps to cultivate, and list potential benefits that result from developing those skills. We then provide rubrics for measuring items that students require to be successful with information fluency's aspects.

## Ask

Ask involves compiling a list of critical questions about what knowledge or data learners seek. Students have any number of uses for information acquisition, but whatever the purpose, the information still must be relevant, accurate, and applicable.

The key here is to ask good questions because that's how to get good answers. Having specific questions about the subject matter or information quest will lead learners on the right paths. Asking good questions trains their minds to think critically and search for relevant and useful data. It also helps them unearth the most valuable information sources in their personal knowledge quests. The skills that students develop in the ask stage, and the beneficial opportunities and possibilities that utilizing each creates, include the following.

- Understanding the problem:
    - Gives the problem the proper context
    - Makes searching for information easier and more focused
    - Eliminates the dangers of flying blind
    - Leads to hearing unique perspectives from others
- Identifying key words:
    - Helps learners identify and verbalize the problem
    - Provides better understanding of the information quest's purpose
    - Helps learners narrow down their search for information
- Forming exploratory questions:
    - Promotes critical thinking and a deeper understanding of the problem
    - Uncovers surprising things about a problem that learners may not have been aware of
    - Guides learners in exploring and approaching the problem fully and from multiple perspectives
- Brainstorming and lateral thinking:
    - Involves the entire team and facilitates a discussion of the problem from multiple viewpoints
    - Helps learners turn problems into opportunities
    - Promotes generation of creative ideas and opinions, which is essential to a collaborative problem-solving process
- Understanding ethical issues:
    - Develops thinking habits based on empathy and compassion
    - Urges learners to consider a problem or issue's far-reaching effects
    - Guides learners toward creating ethical solutions
    - Lets learners empathize with other professional, creative, or cultural viewpoints
- Listening deeply, viewing wisely, and speaking critically:
    - Develops exceptional communication skills
    - Encourages consideration of an issue from various viewpoints, and guards against bias
    - Leads to working toward a solution that benefits everyone
    - Incorporates a broad understanding of human nature and behavior

- Filtering out informational white noise:
  - Develops the important analysis skill of recognizing spurious or unnecessary aspects of information
  - Helps learners separate and organize data for engineering the solution
  - Teaches learners to sort through informational clutter and make sense of large amounts of data
- Sharing personal knowledge and experience:
  - Lets learners share expertise and experience that can be valuable to the solution's success
  - Develops communication and willingness to be open without fear of judgment or ridicule in a supportive environment
  - Allows for an equal measure of both teaching and learning opportunities
  - Lets learners empathize with other professional, creative, or cultural viewpoints

# Acquire

This stage involves accessing and collecting informational materials from the most appropriate digital and nondigital sources. It's also about knowing where to look and understanding that the information won't always be in one location. Students must be sure to use many sources. The Internet, ebooks, articles, libraries, videos, and people in a chosen area of knowledge will provide learners with many different avenues for finding information. The skills that students develop in the acquire stage, and the beneficial opportunities and possibilities that utilizing each creates, include the following.

- Determining where the information is:
  - Teaches effective search skills
  - Familiarizes students with how to access and manage multiple sources of digital and nondigital information
- Determining the skills needed to find the information:
  - Fosters new abilities while acquiring information that can aid learners on other projects and challenges
  - Helps students learn how to find and obtain information ethically
  - Pushes students to expand their range of awareness in the ways information is accessed and used in the digital world
- Skimming, scanning, and scouring resources for data:
  - Increases proficiency through practice of these techniques, which helps with future information quests

- Develops and reinforces organizational skills
- Gives students the ability to determine at a glance what is useful

- Prioritizing search strategies:
  - Helps students decide what information to scrutinize and analyze first
  - Allows learners to call on other team members and delegate data searches, with an accountability system in place for reporting findings
  - Makes the information-gathering process move more quickly
  - Teaches methods for accessing multiple information sources

- Taking smart notes:
  - Trains students to be better observers and listeners
  - Develops better information-organization skills
  - Encourages learners not to be mechanical writers, but rather to consider their real goals for taking notes on a certain subject
  - Helps students learn to be brief and concise, and focus on what's important

- Filtering:
  - Helps students learn to identify facts to inform their audience so they can shape their own opinions
  - Helps learners present their solutions in a more unbiased manner
  - Helps to differentiate fact from opinion
  - Identifies facts that are central to properly supporting the ideas in students' solutions

- Knowing when to go back to the ask stage:
  - Helps learners understand that the fluencies aren't linear processes, but cyclical ones that allow them to revisit each stage if needed
  - Helps learners reconnect with the purpose for their knowledge quest
  - Allows learners to search for new information upon discovering something new about the problem that they didn't consider before

# Analyze

Once learners have collected all the raw data, they must authenticate, organize, and arrange them. This stage also involves ascertaining whether information is true and distinguishing the good from the bad.

Learners must train themselves to know good from bad and right from wrong when dealing with information. When it comes to online content, a percentage of that free information can be spurious. All data require thorough scrutiny and organization. Think of it as a background check on each bit of data that a learner collects.

Many search results display similar threads, or common concepts, that point to repeated experience and commonalities in that field of knowledge that are accepted across a broad range of sources. Some sources share more similarities than others, and the more obscure facts suddenly start to take a back seat to those that multiple sources more often agree on. This isn't foolproof, but it's just one of the many ways that facts about what learners seek can begin to reveal themselves. Depending on the scope of the project or task, learners may spend a lot of time moving between the acquiring and analyzing stages. Don't worry; that's a good thing! The skills that students develop in the analyze stage, and the beneficial opportunities and possibilities that utilizing each creates, include the following.

- Organizing, triangulating, and summarizing:
  - Allows learners to begin seeing what information they can discard
  - Helps learners discern any relevant patterns that may emerge within the data
  - Helps learners find the most logical categorizations for their information
  - Teaches learners to summarize the most pertinent and useful points
  - Allows learners to see what they might still be missing
- Working independently and collaboratively:
  - Hones learners' teamwork skills and ability to interact with others
  - Lets learners put their own theories into practice both inside and outside the team environment
  - Teaches learners how to be responsible for themselves and others in the process of analyzing information for the problem
- Checking for relevance and distinguishing between useful and superficial sources:
  - Helps learners determine the useful data from the irrelevant or spurious data
  - Allows learners to whittle down their information database into more manageable quantities
  - Teaches learners to have a critical eye when analyzing information
  - Allows learners to begin to quickly see what data are most important in that moment

- Differentiating fact from opinion:
  - Helps learners determine facts hidden in large amounts of what is mostly free information from varied sources
  - Allows learners to formulate their own opinions from facts instead of simply relying on someone else's viewpoints
  - Helps learners avoid using falsely generated facts or hearsay when organizing and utilizing data
- Assessing the data currency:
  - Ensures information is up to date
  - Teaches learners to cross-check and verify publication dates for currency
  - Helps learners avoid using irrelevant, outdated, or obsolete information
- Examining data for underlying meaning and bias:
  - Allows learners to determine if sources are borrowing from each other
  - Teaches learners to evaluate data and uncover their deeper relevance to the problem
  - Encourages a neutral stance among biases and allows learners to consider all sides of the issue in a piece of information
- Determining when data answer the original question:
  - Lets learners recognize which parts of data and information actually address the problem
  - Leads learners to re-examine some data and discard them if necessary
  - Helps students learn to document their progress when they find data relevant to their solutions, saving them work later on
- Identifying incomplete information:
  - Encourages learners to search deeply and think critically to find missing pieces of data
  - Urges learners to consider the relevancy of the information's source
  - Helps students learn how information fits together and harmonizes as they approach the application of knowledge for the solution
- Documenting and taking notes to determine authenticity:
  - Teaches the importance of checking sources for credibility and for viability
  - Develops exceptional communication skills
  - Ensures authentic information that is vital to the solution's success

- Using probability, trends, and best guesses:
    - Helps learners understand how some of the most well-used sources may not necessarily be the best, but may still contain useful information
    - Helps learners understand how quickly and rapidly shared information can change or become outdated
    - Teaches learners to make the best estimations possible based on the data
- Turning data into knowledge and wisdom:
    - Encourages learners to revisit the ask or acquire stages to fill in missing data
    - Indicates that students have learned things of value and importance during their information quest
    - Hones learners' ability to apply the information to current and future challenges in a practical way
    - Gives learners a chance to share their newfound wisdom to help others

# Apply

So what do students do with the information they have obtained? Once they have collected and verified the data, and have finally created a solution, they must practically apply the knowledge within the context of the original purpose for the information quest. All that valuable information isn't worth anything if one doesn't do anything with it. After all the hard work asking, acquiring, and analyzing, students must apply what they have learned to their original problem or challenge to make that knowledge work for them.

Remember that information fluency, along with all the other fluencies, is a cyclical process by nature. If students don't answer the question or conquer the challenge in this final phase, it's time to back up a few steps and try again. Don't be alarmed, because this isn't failure—it's a process that learners sometimes must revisit, and that's perfectly natural. The skills that students develop in the apply stage, and the beneficial opportunities and possibilities that utilizing each creates, include the following.

- Turning data into personal knowledge:
    - Infuses learners with a desire to see the problem effectively solved to the best of everyone's ability
    - Indicates that learners understand the information and use it to its full potential
    - Allows learners to share the knowledge with others who may be in need of it

- Applying the knowledge practically:
  - Gives learners a stake in the process, because they want to make sure their hard work has paid off
  - Shows learners whether the knowledge they use is effective
  - Encourages revisiting previous stages in order to revise the process if necessary
- Creating and utilizing products and projects:
  - Demonstrates knowledge application as well as creativity
  - Lets learners consider different projects to use in delivering their knowledge
  - Teaches learners skills in various media as they create different products
  - Brings about a range of different ideas for solutions through teamwork

# Assess

Assess is a reflective stage in students' journeys. Here they look back at the steps they took to find what they were looking for. They also take a look at what the proper application of their knowledge has produced. It involves open and lively discussions about how they could have made the problem-solving journey more efficient, and how they could apply their solution to challenges of a similar nature.

Is the problem solved? Is the question answered? Is the challenge met? How could learners have streamlined their own process and made it more efficient? Questions of this nature are good ones to consider in discussions for this phase. Even after all is said and done, students can still ask critical questions and find new challenges to look forward to. The skills that students develop in the assess stage, and the beneficial opportunities and possibilities that utilizing each creates, include the following.

- Asking questions about the information or process:
  - Pushes everyone on the team to think critically about what they've accomplished
  - Allows learners to share their own opinions and viewpoints constructively
  - Allows learners to reflect on what they have learned on their problem-solving journey and how it has helped them and others
  - Gives learners insights into how they have bonded with others in the process
- Determining and debriefing pros and cons:
  - Allows learners to determine as a group the areas in the process where they could have done some things differently or more efficiently
  - Provides opportunities to discover ways to improve or revise the product

- • Allows learners to revisit the previous stages and obtain new insights
- • Internalizing and transferring new learning:
  - • Makes the learning stick—the more learners practice this process, the more unconscious or fluent it becomes
  - • Gives learners a chance to see how they can apply the knowledge to similar situations and circumstances
  - • Allows learners to begin to see problems as opportunities for greater learning

# Information Fluency in Schools

Following are exemplars of inquiry- and project-based lessons that cultivate information fluency. We've provided samples that cover a variety of grade levels and subjects to ensure all readers have access to relevant, applicable examples. Readers can find the full lessons as well as the activities and assessment resources on the Solution Fluency Activity Planner (https://solutionfluency.com). See the extensive rubrics at the end of this chapter (figures 4.1–4.5, pages 67–72) for tools to facilitate assessment of these and other information fluency lessons.

## Idol History (Primary School)

**Essential question:** What are the most significant contributions and ideas people have made to society in the past?

**Subjects:** History, language arts, design, theater

**Scenario:** Throughout history there have been many individuals who have become famous for their landmark accomplishments. If you were to make your own choice from a list of famous historical figures, who would you choose as being the best?

Choose someone from a list of great historical figures, research their accomplishments, and make a presentation to a panel of judges about who you've chosen and why you consider that person the best choice for "greatest person in history." The more creative, imaginative, and informative you can be the better!

## Gratitude Group (Primary School)

**Essential question:** How could you use a public event to create awareness and express your appreciation of the people in your community?

**Subjects:** Language arts, design, social studies, mathematics

**Scenario:** Take a moment and think about the people who work to make the community strong through the services they provide to its economy. If you had one day to create a celebration to show these people how much you and your community appreciate them, what would you come up with?

Create a unique community celebration showing appreciation for your community leaders and their day-to-day efforts. Use research about expressing thanks in cultures around the world, and make something to show your community how much it matters!

## Lead the Way (Middle School)

**Essential question:** What characteristics make up a good leader, and why are good leaders important in a society?

**Subjects:** Language arts, history, technology, media studies

**Scenario:** Good leaders are important to society. They inspire us, guide us, and help us become better people. Imagine that you're a famous actor or singer who is known for doing a lot of charity work all over the world, and you've recently been asked to do an interview on a popular show.

The topic is "what makes a good leader?" With some classmates, you'll create an interview scenario. Write the script and play different roles, and either record the interview as a live radio interview or capture it on video. Time to take the lead!

## Party Planners (Middle School)

**Essential question:** How do caterers use proportional reasoning to determine costs and quantities for catering events?

**Subjects:** Mathematics, economics, design, technology

**Scenario:** Catering isn't just about great food. It's a busy profession that takes patience, planning, and people skills. And of course, you've got to have a good head for numbers. For you, that's a piece of cake!

You're part of a catering company that is covering a wedding reception. You'll be seating 175 guests. Decide on a five-course menu including various beverages and the wedding cake. You'll be creating actual recipes requiring exact measurements, and also creating a budget for the bash. Time to plan the ultimate party!

## Green Gears (High School)

**Essential question:** How can we use waste products to counteract the effects of consuming our conventional fuel sources?

**Subjects:** Science, mathematics, design, environmental studies, technology

**Scenario:** We're looking to a future where alternative fuel sources remedy many of our environmental issues, such as waste and recycling. With a little ingenuity and some extensive research and experimentation, you can create a solution to benefit us all!

Come up with your own machine that runs on an alternative fuel source. Work in groups and research the innovations that have been discovered in this field as inspiration for your own designs. How will your creation work, and how will it serve humanity?

### The Future Is Now (High School)

**Essential question:** How is our vision of the future affected by the world today?

**Subjects:** Science, technology, language arts, media studies

**Scenario:** All generations have a unique and often fantastical vision of how the world of tomorrow will be. Look twenty years into the future from now—what do you see, and how would you describe it?

Create a presentation that describes a vision of the future in vivid and creative detail. Tell about everything that you see and do for one day in this future world. Use digital rendering and creative presentation tools to bring your idea to life as a digital media creation of your choice. Share your vision of tomorrow!

## Rubrics for Information Fluency

We provide the following rubrics as examples for evaluating student performance on items that contribute to information fluency, including descriptions of what student performance or work products might look like at each phase of the essential fluencies framework.

| ? Ask | Phase 1 (awareness, connection, remembering) | Phase 2 (understanding, applying) | Phase 3 (analyzing, evaluating) | Phase 4 (evaluating, creating) |
|---|---|---|---|---|
| Defines information needs, identifies key words, and forms questions around them | • Identifies some key words and states basic questions to collect some pertinent information for the task based on the definition; some questions and key words are redundant or irrelevant; many questions are closed | • Identifies a suitable range of relevant key words and uses these to develop some probing and inquiring questions; most questions are task-focused and will yield useful information; there are few closed questions | • Breaks the problem down into its component parts and identifies a suitable range of relevant key words<br>• Uses these component parts to develop a range of inquiry questions that are focused on the problem and enable effective and efficient access to information | • Identifies a suitable range of relevant key words and uses these to develop a range of inquiry questions that are focused on the definition and that enable effective and efficient access to a broad and suitable range of information sources<br>• Reflects on and refines the questions as required |

*Visit **go.SolutionTree.com/assessment** for a free reproducible version of this figure.*

**Figure 4.1: Information fluency assessment rubric—Ask.**

| Acquire | Phase 1 (awareness, connection, remembering) | Phase 2 (understanding, applying) | Phase 3 (analyzing, evaluating) | Phase 4 (evaluating, creating) |
|---|---|---|---|---|
| **Accesses suitable information sources** | • Accesses the provided resources | • Accesses a range of resources, including and beyond provided options, which are mostly suitable and authoritative | • Accesses a range of select suitable and authoritative resources, which could include appropriate primary sources | • Creatively accesses a broad range of suitable and imaginative resources, which could include primary sources |
| **Demonstrates effective strategies for recording processes and results** | • Sometimes uses suitable processes or strategies to document the results of the research; information is recorded but lacks structure or organization | • Uses suitable processes or strategies to document the results of the research; information is organized to allow access and recall<br>• Often includes suitable tags, key words, and descriptions | • Uses suitable processes, strategies, and technologies to document the process and results of the research; information is suitably organized and structured to allow easy access, recall, and modification of search or research parameters as required<br>• Includes suitable comments and reflections on the validity and accuracy of data sources<br>• Includes suitable tags, key words, and descriptions | • not applicable |
| **Accesses suitable secondary information sources**<br><br>**Demonstrates effective search and filtering strategies** | • Uses basic unmodified searches and often uses sentences rather than key words<br>• Will use text language to structure searches<br>• Is largely limited to researching from one medium | • Accesses a range of sources that are mostly suitable and authoritative<br>• Sometimes accesses several different media (Internet, journals, newspapers, texts, reference books, and so on)<br>• Selects and enters suitable key words<br>• Sometimes modifies the search using the advanced features of search engines to refine the search<br>• Frequently reviews and modifies search to produce appropriate results | • Systematically accesses a variety of suitable resources to provide appropriate information<br>• Selects suitable key words and uses the advanced features of search engines to refine the search<br>• Collates the critical information into component parts, checking that information is collected for each aspect or component<br>• Can review and modify search modifiers to produce appropriate results | • Accesses a variety of suitable resources to provide relevant, authoritative, and appropriate information<br>• Selects suitable key words and modifies these with Boolean operators<br>• Uses the advanced features of search engines to refine the search, which could include date range, domain, country, language, and so on<br>• Can critically review and modify search modifiers to produce appropriate results |

| Acquire | Phase 1 (awareness, connection, remembering) | Phase 2 (understanding, applying) | Phase 3 (analyzing, evaluating) | Phase 4 (evaluating, creating) |
|---|---|---|---|---|
| **Accesses suitable primary information sources** <br><br> **Demonstrates effective research and interview strategies** | • Prepares some closed questions and few open-ended questions, some of which could be answered from secondary sources | • Completes some secondary research to prepare for primary research or interview <br> • Prepares some open-ended questions, which are focused on the topic and cannot be answered from secondary sources <br> • Is suitably prepared to record the responses accurately | • Completes secondary research to prepare for primary research or interview <br> • Prepares suitable open-ended questions, which address the component parts or aspects of the problem, are focused on the topic, and cannot be easily answered from secondary sources <br> • Has a realistic number of questions and is suitably prepared to record the responses; questions are, where required, challenging and probing but appropriate | • Arranges access to secondary sources who are recognized authorities in their field <br> • Completes extensive secondary research to prepare for primary research or interview <br> • Prepares creative questions, which are focused on the topic and cannot be answered from secondary sources <br> • Has a realistic number of questions, organized into a suitable structure or flow, which will lead logically through the sequence of questions <br> • Is suitably prepared to record the responses accurately |

*Visit **go.SolutionTree.com/assessment** for a free reproducible version of this figure.*

**Figure 4.2: Information fluency assessment rubric—Acquire.**

| Analyze | Phase 1 (awareness, connection, remembering) | Phase 2 (understanding, applying) | Phase 3 (analyzing, evaluating) | Phase 4 (evaluating, creating) |
|---|---|---|---|---|
| Validates information—separates fact from opinion, recognizes bias, identifies incomplete information, and uses effective strategies to analyze and authenticate information and make it useful | • Does not validate information for accuracy or factual basis | • Applies basic techniques for validating information sources<br>• Will sometimes include multiple related information sources, but has not made a critical judgment on whether these should be included | • Applies a variety of suitable techniques to critically evaluate each information source's validity<br>• Provides multiple information sources to support critical information<br>• Can break down information into component parts and compare different elements' validity<br>• Can recognize bias and opinion | • Applies a variety of suitable techniques to critically evaluate each information source's validity<br>• Provides multiple information sources to support critical information<br>• Can break down information into component parts and evaluate different elements' validity<br>• Recognizes bias and opinion and critically applies the information while considering them<br>• Can justify the process undertaken and the information's validity |

*Visit **go.SolutionTree.com/assessment** for a free reproducible version of this figure.*

**Figure 4.3: Information fluency assessment rubric—Analyze.**

| Apply | Phase 1 (awareness, connection, remembering) | Phase 2 (understanding, applying) | Phase 3 (analyzing, evaluating) | Phase 4 (evaluating, creating) |
|---|---|---|---|---|
| **Effectively applies knowledge within the originally required context** | • Makes some use of the collected information; much of the information is in its original form; there is little refinement of the information | • Applies the collected information to develop a broad understanding of the task, its background, and so on<br><br>• Will sometimes recognize areas of limited information or validity and refine searches or instigate new ones | • Uses the collected and collated information to structure the task<br><br>• Reviews the information and makes critical judgments on the depth and breadth of knowledge required for the task<br><br>• Will recognize areas of limited information or validity and refine searches or undertake new searches to correct them<br><br>• Includes some evaluation of the information's validity and accuracy | • Creatively uses the processed information to structure the task<br><br>• Critically reviews the information and makes critical judgments on the depth and breadth of information required for the task<br><br>• Applies information from multiple sources and media using imaginative and focused strategies and techniques<br><br>• Recognizes areas of limited information or validity and will refine or undertake new searches to correct them<br><br>• Includes evaluation of the information's validity and accuracy |
| **Effectively processes data into information** | • Often presents data in a basic unprocessed format or with minimum processing; there are obvious errors, and little relevant error checking and validation have taken place | • Processes the data collected into suitable forms<br><br>• Has accuracy in processing and some errors<br><br>• Will sometimes undertake error checking | • Processes the data collected into suitable forms<br><br>• Has accuracy in processing and few errors<br><br>• Will often undertake error checking<br><br>• Often reviews information to validate its accuracy<br><br>• Is able to analyze some of the limitations of the processed data (information) | • Creatively processes the data collected into easily accessible forms that highlight the data<br><br>• Has a high degree of accuracy in processing and error checking<br><br>• Critically reviews information to validate its accuracy<br><br>• Is able to evaluate the limitations of the processed data (information)<br><br>• Is able to identify complex relationships and patterns |

**Figure 4.4: Information fluency assessment rubric—Apply.** continued →

| Apply | Phase 1 (awareness, connection, remembering) | Phase 2 (understanding, applying) | Phase 3 (analyzing, evaluating) | Phase 4 (evaluating, creating) |
|---|---|---|---|---|
| Cites and records all references accurately when gathering information | • Recalls a simple list of resources used with little or no formatting or processing | • Applies suitable citation techniques to develop an appropriate bibliography | • Consistently and accurately uses suitable methods to provide a detailed, complete bibliography of information sources<br>• Suitably acknowledges primary information sources<br>• Will seek permission to use resources where appropriate | • not applicable |
| Ethically obtains information | • Recalls information from a variety of sources with little consideration for permission, copyright, or intellectual property | • Applies and abides by fair use policies, and uses suitable techniques to access suitably licensed resources | • Seeks permission to use resources<br>• Abides by fair use policies, and uses suitable techniques to access suitably licensed resources | • not applicable |

*Visit **go.SolutionTree.com/assessment** for a free reproducible version of this figure.*

| Assess | Phase 1 (awareness, connection, remembering) | Phase 2 (understanding, applying) | Phase 3 (analyzing, evaluating) | Phase 4 (evaluating, creating) |
|---|---|---|---|---|
| Reflects critically on application of information and the gathering process, making revisions for improvement | • Provides reflection that is often superficial and incomplete<br>• May offer some next steps, but does not link them to the reflection | • Can provide some reflection on the different stages of the process undertaken; reflection is generally appropriate and fair<br>• Identifies some areas for further research | • Can provide a suitable analysis (stage by stage) and some evaluation of the process undertaken; reflection is thoughtful and appropriate<br>• Provides a reflection and clear next steps based on the evaluation<br>• Identifies some areas where further research may be needed | • Can offer a clear and concise evaluation of the process undertaken; reflection is fair, thoughtful, deliberate, and appropriate<br>• Provides a detailed reflection and clear next steps based on the evaluation<br>• Identifies areas where further research is required and takes action on them |

*Visit **go.SolutionTree.com/assessment** for a free reproducible version of this figure.*

**Figure 4.5: Information fluency assessment rubric—Assess.**

While information fluency may seem to echo the solution fluency's discover aspect, the two are applied in different ways. Solution fluency is the process most appropriate for project-based learning, while information fluency stands alone as the guiding process for inquiry-based learning. The aspects of information fluency are essential not only for students' ability to seek and gain the information they need but also to evaluate the information's accuracy, relevance, and credibility.

# Guiding Questions

Before moving to the next chapter, answer the following questions as an individual or with your school team.

1. What does it mean to be information fluent? Can you recall instances in which you have practiced some information fluency skills?

2. Why is information fluency so important to apply when searching online for facts and data?

3. What major transformations in our culture have facilitated the need for having information fluency?

4. Why is it important to ask critical, probing questions when searching for information to apply to a problem or task?

# chapter 5

# Creativity Fluency

The capacity to be creative resides within all of us. It is inherent to our nature and has existed as a fire within us since we became a part of this world. We look to the stars, and we dream. We put pen to paper, and we create entire worlds to lose ourselves in. We perceive beautiful giants living within blocks of rough-hewn marble, waiting to be freed. We gaze on blank canvases or the cold and barren ceilings of cathedrals and forge masterpieces that live on for generations.

Today, our canvases are computer and tablet screens, and we can instantaneously share our creations across a world without barriers. Indeed we are creative, and this is a process that any teacher can impart to any student.

We have engineered this process into what we call creativity fluency. Artistic proficiency adds meaning through design, art, and storytelling in this method. It is about using innovative design to add value to a product's function through its form. We define the creativity fluency aspects as the 5Is: (1) identify, (2) inspire, (3) interpolate, (4) imagine, and (5) inspect. In this chapter, we will describe these aspects, note some skills each helps to cultivate, and list potential benefits that result from developing those skills. We then provide rubrics for measuring items that students require to be successful with the creativity fluency aspects.

## Identify

Identify involves distinguishing the elements and the criteria of the desired outcome. It's about figuring out what students need to create and what limitations or restrictions they face. They begin by asking what the task is and what they want to create. The skills that students develop in the identify stage, and the beneficial opportunities and possibilities that utilizing each creates, include the following.

- Understanding the problem:
  - Gives the problem the proper context
  - Makes searching for data and information easier and more focused

- Eliminates the dangers of flying blind
- Leads to hearing unique perspectives from others
- Identifying key words:
  - Helps learners identify and verbalize the desired outcome
  - Allows learners to better understand the purpose of their quest for an idea
  - Helps learners narrow down their search for inspirational elements
- Forming key word questions:
  - Promotes critical thinking and a deeper understanding of learners' creative wishes
  - Guides learners in exploring the key words for sources of inspiration
- Brainstorming and lateral thinking:
  - Lets learners examine their desired outcomes from multiple angles and viewpoints
  - Helps learners turn problems into opportunities
  - Generates ideas and opinions, an important part of the creative process
- Understanding ethical issues:
  - Develops thinking habits based on empathy and compassion
  - Urges learners to consider a problem or issue's far-reaching effects
  - Guides learners toward creating ethical solutions
  - Lets learners empathize with other professional, creative, or cultural viewpoints
- Listening deeply, viewing wisely, and speaking critically:
  - Develops exceptional communication skills and habits of mind
  - Encourages consideration of an idea from various viewpoints, and guards against bias
  - Leads to working toward creating something that benefits everyone
  - Incorporates a broad understanding of human nature and behavior
- Sharing personal knowledge and experience:
  - Lets learners share expertise and experience that can be valuable to the success of their creative ideas
  - Develops communication and willingness to be open in a supportive environment without fear of judgment or ridicule
  - Allows learners to empathize with other professional, creative, or cultural viewpoints

# Inspire

In this stage, the adventure begins by stimulating learners' creativity with rich sensory input. This involves any action, encounter, or lively conversation that fires their imagination. This phase is all about feeding the creative appetite.

From where do students draw their inspiration? Inspiration can come from old memories, visualization exercises, books and magazines, museums and galleries, their favorite websites or music, or stimulating conversations with good friends. Thousands of inspiration sources surround us every day of our lives, and any of these may trigger an idea. The skills that students develop in the inspire stage, and the beneficial opportunities and possibilities that utilizing each creates, include the following.

- Moving beyond what is known:
  - Encourages learners to invite in new experiences to enrich their minds
  - Introduces learners to new ideas, opinions, and perceptions
  - Teaches learners never to be afraid of what they don't know
  - Allows for discovery of hidden talents and abilities learners didn't know they had
- Using familiar and unfamiliar sources:
  - Creates new abilities that can aid learners with other projects and challenges
  - Provides a sense of comfort and allows learners to prepare for the unfamiliar with confidence
  - Broadens learners' awareness of new media and how they appeal to different people in different ways
- Seeing new possibilities:
  - Allows learners to see more than one outcome and solution
  - Helps learners see current outcomes from different perspectives
  - Makes learners more invested in the process of solidifying their ideas as they discover more and more possible journeys
  - Conditions learners to constantly strive for a vision and never give up
- Playing with ideas:
  - Promotes creativity
  - Encourages learners to be fearless and exploratory with ideas
  - Has a positive effect on the emotions and keeps the brain healthy
  - Helps form new neural connections

- Experimenting and imagining:
  - Allows learners to express their true inner desires and hopes for the intended outcome
  - Opens up new paths for learning and discovering
  - Gives learners a chance to predict both the successful and the potentially flawed outcomes

# Interpolate

The left brain analyzes the sensory input from the right brain, searching for patterns, alternative meanings, and high-level abstractions to connect the dots. To interpolate means to find a structured pattern within known information. Somewhere in all that randomness, a connection awaits discovery. The skills that students develop in the interpolate stage, and the beneficial opportunities and possibilities that utilizing each creates, include the following.

- Recognizing patterns:
  - Allows learners to predict what could happen next or what might be revealed next in a logical progression
  - Trains learners to use their senses and compare new experiences with previous ones to see how they can use them
  - Prepares learners to make intelligent decisions
- Identifying connections and relationships:
  - Allows learners to make connections to prior experiences and apply them to new ideas
  - Helps learners determine what makes these connections effective
  - Helps to structure thought processes to gain further inspiration and develop new ideas
- Combining opposing concepts and elements:
  - Forms new ideas, experiences, and possibilities
  - Allows learners to connect unrelated elements or concepts harmoniously to engage critical-thinking skills
  - Integrates opposing ideas for the purpose of forming new and better ones in order to fuel personal success
- Thinking laterally about existing knowledge:
  - Helps learners discover unique solutions and possibilities
  - Trains learners to see the familiar in a new way, which can spark creative ideas

- Frees learners from limited thinking, and allows them to work in a mental space in which there is always a solution or answer

# Imagine

This is the ultimate synthesis between the previous stages of inspire and interpolate. These stages' unification results in the birth of an idea—the aha moment. After all the extraneous information is gone, learners start to zero in on a possible solution. This phase of true diligence allows students to almost see, feel, touch, or taste the solution they're after and keep after it. The moment comes when the inspire and interpolate stages come together to form the ideal idea. The skills that students develop in the imagine stage, and the beneficial opportunities and possibilities that utilizing each creates, include the following.

- Forming mental images, sensations, and concepts:
  - Exercises learners' imagination and pushes their creative potential
  - Encourages learners to move beyond the restrictions of their senses while still drawing on their personal experiences with them
- Giving meaning to experiences:
  - Involves recalling past experiences and articulating them
  - Adds personal value to the idea or concept learners are working with
  - Lets learners put their hearts, spirits, and minds into what they create
  - Allows learners to affect others positively through their enthusiasm
- Constructing with creative media:
  - Puts learners in a leadership role so they can create and synthesize their vision freely
  - Allows learners to work with different creative media (storytelling, art and graphic design, music, poetry, video, and so on)
  - Shows learners the creative results of their efforts, and helps them develop a sense of accomplishment and responsibility

# Inspect

In order to make a new creative idea become a reality, students ask themselves questions about the idea's effectiveness and feasibility, and if it can be accomplished within an existing time frame and budget. Students may discover that the answer to these questions is no, and the idea may not be suitable after all. It's a good idea to keep that idea for future use, or it may simply need refinement and adjustment. The skills that students develop in the inspect stage, and processes, and the beneficial opportunities and possibilities that utilizing each creates, include the following.

- Examining the product and the process:
    - Lets learners recognize how their ideas actually address the challenge
    - Leads learners to re-examine some of the steps they took to determine where they could have made better choices
    - Gives learners insight into the creative process's importance, and also demonstrates how any creation starts with an idea
- Comparing and contrasting with the original purpose:
    - Allows learners to see if their ideas answer the questions that led them to begin the creative process
    - Gives rise to new concepts and ideas to apply to the same challenge or to similar challenges
    - Reminds learners why the product and process are relevant and meaningful
- Internalizing and applying the new idea:
    - Makes the learning stick—the more learners practice this process, the more fluent they become
    - Gives learners a chance to see how they can apply the new idea to similar situations and circumstances
    - Allows learners to consider the idea's time and budgetary implications
- Re-examining and revising the idea:
    - Gives learners a fresh look at how they could improve or enhance an idea
    - Reinforces the reality that creativity fluency, like other fluencies, is a cyclical process
    - Lets learners discover the limits of an idea's potential and then work to exceed them
    - Gives birth to new creative ideas and concepts

# Creativity Fluency in Schools

Following are exemplars of inquiry- and project-based lessons that cultivate creativity fluency. We've provided samples that cover a variety of grade levels and subjects to ensure all readers have access to relevant, applicable examples. Readers can find the full lessons as well as the activities and assessment resources on the Solution Fluency Activity Planner (https://solutionfluency.com). See the extensive rubrics at the end of this chapter (figures 5.1–5.5, pages 83–87) for tools to facilitate assessment of these and other creativity fluency lessons.

## Magic Mystery (Primary School)

**Essential question:** How can we use art and storytelling to help solve mysteries?

**Subjects:** Language arts, arts, scientific reasoning, design

**Scenario:** Exploring the unknown is very exciting, and solving the problem becomes an incredible reward. Do you have what it takes to create a mystery? Let's find out!

Create a mystery story to train new detectives in solving crimes. Act out your tales using props for the new detectives in training (the rest of the class). Once the stories are created, challenge the rest of the observing detectives to solve them using clues, evidence, observations, and a detailed time line summarizing the crime and its participants. Now the game is afoot!

## The Light Painters (Primary School)

**Essential question:** How can you combine your knowledge of mathematics, art, and design to help resolve a problem?

**Subjects:** Geography, science, language arts, technology

**Scenario:** A heavy storm recently struck your city and ravaged a prominent stained glass window in a landmark church. Rather than build a replica of the broken window, the church council has called for artists to submit design templates for a brand new window.

You have a good design sense and a talent for creating geometric patterns. Why not try your hand at creating a design? Work in pairs or groups to create the most remarkable stained glass draft you can think of, using mathematics and fun research tools. Then present your design to the council and show them your amazing work! Create a light-infused work of art!

## FUNderwater (Middle School)

**Essential question:** How would you explain the stages of the water cycle using illustration and animation techniques?

**Subjects:** Science, graphic arts, design, environmental studies, language arts

**Scenario:** The water cycle is food for the Earth and all its inhabitants, from the smallest organism to the largest mammal alive. If you had the chance, how would you both entertain and educate younger kids about this amazing process?

Bring the magic of Earth's water cycle to a younger audience. You get to explain how the water cycle works and why it's important to life on our planet in a creative and engaging animated cartoon, comic storyboard, or original live skit designed for a children's educational science program.

## Design Star (Middle School)

Lessons that cultivate multiple fluencies appear in each applicable fluency.

**Essential question:** How can interior designers use mathematics to bring their visions to life?

**Subjects:** Mathematics, language arts, design, art, technology

**Scenario:** A successful designer is one who has an innate sense of style and a solid mathematical foundation. Could you succeed in the design industry? This is a great way to find out!

Select a messy or uninspiring space to redesign, and build a scale model to display your vision. Plan the new design and build a diorama that displays the space's major lengths, widths, and heights to scale. Then put your design mojo to work!

You can create a video or slideshow that captures the design process along with before shots of the chosen space and after shots of your scale model. Design your perfect space!

## Mock Doc (High School)

**Essential question:** What goes on behind the scenes when making a documentary about an important topic?

**Subjects:** Language arts, design, media, technology, filmmaking

**Scenario:** Documentaries demonstrate an intimate knowledge about a particular subject, something that the creator cares very deeply about. Think about the documentaries you've seen on TV that you really enjoyed. What about them gave you that reaction?

Working in groups, pick a topic of interest to yourselves and create a full-fledged documentary on this amazing subject. Demonstrate your expertise about the steps involved in research and production, and get to know more about how documentaries are designed to be both informative and compelling!

## Break the Silence (High School)

**Essential question:** How can we express ourselves about important issues in ways other than simply verbalizing them?

**Subjects:** Language arts, design, theater, dance, visual arts

**Scenario:** There is always something that we are not comfortable talking about. How would you express yourself and get people to listen using more than just normal speech? Are you a singer, songwriter, or both? Are you a dancer? An artist or a poet? Time to let it shine!

Draw on special talents and abilities you have (and that others may not know about) to express yourself about an issue that concerns you. Use something more than just simple words to bring your ideas and feelings out into the most powerful and creative means of self-expression. Let yourself be heard without fear.

# Rubrics for Creativity Fluency

We provide the following rubrics as examples for evaluating student performance on items that contribute to creativity fluency, including descriptions of what student performance or work products might look like at each phase of the essential fluencies framework.

| ☑️ Identify | Phase 1 (awareness, connection, remembering) | Phase 2 (understanding, applying) | Phase 3 (analyzing, evaluating) | Phase 4 (evaluating, creating) |
|---|---|---|---|---|
| **Clearly defines the requirements and needed outcome or purpose** | • Identifies the outcome | • Identifies and defines the requirements and the core elements of the outcome | • Defines the requirements and needed outcome or purpose and audience<br>• Evaluates the requirements, including the intended outcome of the product, considering some of the causal factors | • Clearly defines the requirements and needed outcome or purpose and audience<br>• Evaluates the rationale behind the requirements in depth, including the intended outcome of the product<br>• Considers a variety of causal factors which might include the psychological and emotional effect of the product |
| **Identifies the audience and considers its needs, preferences, and motivations** | • Identifies the audience | • Identifies and states the audience<br>• Outlines some of the audience's requirements | • Is able to evaluate most of the audience's needs and relate them to the task | • Is able to evaluate, in depth, the audience's needs and to relate them to the task or outcome in detail |
| **Creates a list of key words and descriptors to identify tangible and intangible elements** | • States some key words or concepts | • Identifies and defines the requirements and the core elements of the outcome | • Defines the requirements and needed outcome or purpose and audience<br>• Evaluates the requirements, including the intended outcome of the product, considering some of the causal factors | • Clearly defines the requirements and needed outcome or purpose and audience<br>• Is able to evaluate, in depth, the audience's needs and to relate them to the task or outcome in detail |

*Visit **go.SolutionTree.com/assessment** for a free reproducible version of this figure.*

**Figure 5.1: Creativity fluency assessment rubric—Identify.**

| Inspire | Phase 1 (awareness, connection, remembering) | Phase 2 (understanding, applying) | Phase 3 (analyzing, evaluating) | Phase 4 (evaluating, creating) |
|---|---|---|---|---|
| **Uses familiar and unfamiliar sources; references a wide range of media, source materials, and comparable elements to foster ideas** | • Accesses a range of familiar sources related to the task and records most of them | • Accesses a range of different stimuli<br>• Presents a selection of sources and stimuli, predominantly from those they are familiar with | • Accesses and examines a range of different stimulus material from both familiar and unfamiliar sources, but predominantly or entirely from secondary sources<br>• Has a wide selection of sources and stimuli | • Accesses and critically examines a broad range of different stimulus material from secondary and possibly primary sources, and familiar and unfamiliar sources<br>• Shows creativity in his or her selection of sources and stimuli, often including the unusual and challenging; the stimulus covers an imaginative and wide variety of related and potentially unrelated but useful sources |
| **Critically examines inspiration sources** | • not applicable | • Shows ability to relate his or her selection of stimuli to the task, outcome, and audience | • Shows ability to justify his or her selection of stimuli in relation to the task, intended outcome, and audience | • Shows ability to justify his or her selection or nonselection of stimuli in relation to the task, intended outcome, and audience |

*Visit **go.SolutionTree.com/assessment** for a free reproducible version of this figure.*

**Figure 5.2: Creativity fluency assessment rubric—Inspire.**

| Interpolate | Phase 1 (awareness, connection, remembering) | Phase 2 (understanding, applying) | Phase 3 (analyzing, evaluating) | Phase 4 (evaluating, creating) |
|---|---|---|---|---|
| **Creatively combines elements of different stimuli and sources, personal experiences, and underlying principles of the medium to create a unique creative outcome** | • Views different sources that might apply to the task and definition | • Considers a limited range of sources and some of the underlying rules of the medium as they apply to the task and definition | • Considers different stimuli and sources, his or her personal experiences, and some of the underlying rules of the medium as they apply to the task and definition | • Creatively and imaginatively considers different stimuli and sources, his or her personal experiences and preferences, and the underlying rules of the medium or elements of the material as they apply to the task and definition |
| **Makes connections and recognizes patterns** | • Has some awareness of the underlying rules of the medium | • Can apply the underlying rules of the medium | • Recognizes some patterns and relationships and can apply them to develop a concept, design, or idea that is suitable for the purpose and the audience | • Recognizes patterns and relationships and can apply them creatively to develop a concept, design, or idea that has unique or original qualities that are suitable for the purpose and the audience |
| **Critically reviews inspiration resources for relevancy** | • not applicable | • Offers no or limited explanation of his or her selection | • Offers explanation of his or her selection and its critique | • Critically examines and evaluates, offering a detailed explanation of his or her selection and critique |

*Visit **go.SolutionTree.com/assessment** for a free reproducible version of this figure.*

**Figure 5.3: Creativity fluency assessment rubric—Interpolate.**

| Imagine | Phase 1 (awareness, connection, remembering) | Phase 2 (understanding, applying) | Phase 3 (analyzing, evaluating) | Phase 4 (evaluating, creating) |
|---|---|---|---|---|
| **Consistently connects various source materials to create original products and ideas; demonstrates divergent thinking while considering possible solutions** | • Combines elements of stimulus material to envision a product | • Combines elements of the medium, stimulus material, governing concepts, and rules of the medium to imagine a product suitable for the task and the audience | • Combines some elements of the medium, stimulus material, governing concepts, and rules of the medium (color theory, principles of design, and so on), prior experiences, and personal vision to visualize a product suitable for the task and the audience | • Synthesizes different elements of the medium, stimulus material, governing concepts and rules of the medium (color theory, principles of design, and so on), prior experiences, and personal vision to visualize a unique product suitable for the task and the audience |
| **Combines creative form with technical function to enhance value** | • Considers some of the different requirements of the outcome or product | • Considers most of the different requirements of the outcome or product, which are largely functional | • Considers the different requirements of the outcome or product, which are functional | • Creates an outcome or product that is technically functional and shows critical aesthetic features |
| **Communicates and justifies his or her vision** | • not applicable | • Outlines his or her vision of the product | • Describes the concept and justifies some of his or her design features | • Articulates the concept fluently in a suitable medium (written, oral, pictorial, and so on) and justifies his or her design features with reference to stimulus material, principles, and experience |

*Visit **go.SolutionTree.com/assessment** for a free reproducible version of this figure.*

**Figure 5.4: Creativity fluency assessment rubric—Imagine.**

| ⚖️ **Inspect** | **Phase 1** (awareness, connection, remembering) | **Phase 2** (understanding, applying) | **Phase 3** (analyzing, evaluating) | **Phase 4** (evaluating, creating) |
|---|---|---|---|---|
| Reflects critically on ideas for alignment with original objectives, revising or reconstructing when necessary | • Reviews the concept with some limited reference to the factors or criteria developed in the identify stage | • Reviews the concept and considers some of the factors that have an impact on the concept<br>• Attempts to measure the envisioned concept against some of the criteria developed in the identify stage | • Reviews the concept and considers some of the factors that have an impact on the concept<br>• Measures his or her envisioned concept against most of the criteria developed in the identify stage | • Reviews the concept and considers the diverse factors that have an impact on the success of the concept, which could include feasibility (cost, time, skills, availability of resources, and so on), the audience's requirements, the definition of the purpose of the product or outcome, and so on |
| Communicates selection process effectively | • not applicable | • Outlines his or her decisions and selection process | • Describes his or her decisions and selection process | • Fluently and articulately justifies his or her judgment, critique, decisions, and processes |

*Visit **go.SolutionTree.com/assessment** for a free reproducible version of this figure.*

**Figure 5.5: Creativity fluency assessment rubric—Inspect.**

Creativity is often misunderstood as a mythical or almost psychic phenomenon that one either has, or doesn't. In our experience, creativity is a process—one that can be communicated, cultivated, measured, and improved on. We open unlimited possibilities for our learners by letting go of the creativity myth.

# Guiding Questions

Before moving to the next chapter, answer the following questions as an individual or with your school team.

1. Why is being creative so important to businesses in their bid to create successful and popular products? What edge does creativity give them over their competitors?

2. How do you think the creativity fluency process could be applied to more technical subjects, such as mathematics or science?

3. How can the creativity fluency process benefit those who claim that they are not creative?

4. Can you think of times when you have experienced an aha moment? Where did this moment lead you, and what was the result?

# chapter 6

# Media Fluency

A broad range of readily accessible and increasingly inexpensive digital tools, from cell phones to computers to tablets, now allows us to produce visual and audio-visual content en masse. We have moved beyond simple text-based communication to become a visual society. John Medina (2008) points out in his book *Brain Rules* that the brain processes images over sixty-thousand times faster than it does text. More than 86 billion neurons are dedicated to vision, as well as 70 percent of our sensory receptors (Medina, 2008). As a result, more than 80 percent of the information we receive and decode is received through our eyes. Visual media are largely how we consume information and data, and the trend is only becoming more and more prevalent in our culture.

One of the highest-rated skills our students require in the information age is the ability to create original digital products with a wide array of differing media applications. However, as much as students must know how to do it, they must also be able to determine why it was done. The intended message is just as crucial a piece of the puzzle as the medium chosen to create it. This is the essence of media fluency.

Media fluency includes two aspects we call the 2Ls—(1) listen and (2) leverage, both of which apply to a breakdown of both the medium and the message. In this chapter, we will describe these aspects, note some of the skills each helps to cultivate, and list potential benefits that result from developing those skills. We then provide rubrics for measuring items that students require to be successful with the aspects of media fluency.

## Listen

Listen is about measuring the effectiveness of messages that the media communicate. It's the ability to look critically at a website, video, blog, wiki, TV show, newscast, or video game's content. This involves a careful consideration of both the message and the medium, and being able to decode the real message in the wide range of media available to the average individual. Listen focuses on understanding how users can shape, slant, or even completely misrepresent messages. The skills that students develop in the listen stage for both the message and the medium, and the beneficial opportunities and possibilities that utilizing each creates, include the following.

## Message

We must first separate the message from the medium itself to accurately evaluate the message. When we remove all the media's distractions, what is really being communicated? What are the creators of the message really saying?

- **Verbalizing:** Thinking analytically about what the message is—what is truly being said—and stating the real message clearly and concisely—
  - Teaches learners to avoid complacency and becoming a "victim of media"
  - Trains learners to think critically, analytically, and independently about the messages in media
  - Guides learners toward forming their own opinions
  - Lets learners articulate the true message in their own terms
- **Verifying:** Using skills from information fluency, analyzing and authenticating, separating fact from opinion, and detecting bias—
  - Helps learners identify and differentiate fact from opinion
  - Trains learners to consider the possibility that the message may be opinion masquerading as fact
  - Allows learners to search for deeper meanings by using data research and detection skills inherent in information fluency
  - Shows learners how the message may differ from others' perspectives

## Medium

Looking at the medium involves an analysis of the physical delivery as well as evaluation of the chosen medium's efficacy and appropriateness.

- **Evaluating form:** This is primarily about the design. It includes things like the color scheme, font, unity, balance, white space, lighting, and so on—
  - Trains learners to consider whether the design works harmoniously with the message as intended
  - Helps students learn about the principles of effective graphic design
  - Shows learners that if design elements work as they are meant to, often words and text aren't even necessary
  - Demonstrates how design is intended to invoke feeling and opinion

- **Evaluating flow**: Flow refers to the logical progression within the chosen medium, from beginning to end—

    - Trains learners to notice where the eye is meant to be drawn and where attention is designed to be led

    - Familiarizes learners with multimedia tools' use and effectiveness

    - Introduces learners to the concept of flow in all parts of their everyday lives (arts and entertainment, advertising, marketing, and so on)

    - Shows learners how the message may differ from others' perspectives

- **Evaluating alignment:** If the medium, message, and audience do not align, the message will be ineffective or less effective than it could be—

    - Trains learners to question what the intended audience and purpose are for the communication

    - Leads learners to consider whether the chosen medium was appropriate, or if a different choice would have made better impact

    - Helps learners understand demographic analysis for choosing media

    - Demonstrates how marketing reaches people using various media

# Leverage

Leverage means learning how to communicate effectively and being able to identify the most appropriate medium for delivering a message. For one particular message, a podcast might be the best tool. Other times, a website, a video, or perhaps a printed document or an interactive PDF might be most effective.

In the leverage stage, students select and apply the most appropriate media for the message, considering content, purpose, audience, individual abilities, and any predetermined criteria. As with the listen stage, they consider the message and the medium separately, now using different criteria. We consider these two elements from media creators' perspective rather than viewers.

The skills that students develop in the leverage stage for both the message and the medium, and the beneficial opportunities and possibilities that utilizing each creates, include the following. Note that some opportunities and possible outcomes are listed with more than one skill, as some skills are similar and based on common fundamental concepts.

## *Message*

Always start with the message. The elements to consider are audience, outcome, and content, and students must define them all clearly. Though one leads to another, they do not always occur in the same order. In some cases, for example when you have a fact or news to share, the content will be predetermined and the outcome therefore needs to be considered. In other cases, for example in swaying one's opinion to vote for a specific candidate, the outcome will be predetermined and the content must be considered. In all cases there must be a clear understanding of both the content and the outcome.

- **Considering audience:** The audience's identity is an essential component for students to consider when choosing the most appropriate medium for their message—

  - Guides learners toward making important considerations about their audience demographic (age, gender, culture, and so on)

  - Leads learners to consider the possible necessity for multiple messages

  - Helps learners develop diverse interpersonal communication skills

  - Teaches learners to consider the most effective ways to connect with the broadest range of people

- **Considering outcome:** What learners say is often not as important as how they say it. This is often referred to as tone. It is the tone that will determine how a message will be received and, therefore, the outcome—

  - Leads learners to see that the same information can be presented and interpreted in different ways

  - Develops learners' verbal and nonverbal communication skills

  - Gives learners a deeper understanding of the human psyche through knowing how people react to the same input in different ways

  - Helps learners come to respect the others' opinions

- **Considering content:** The message's substance or content—what they want to say—is another essential component students must consider—

  - Leads learners to carefully consider what they want their audience to understand or to learn from their message

  - Helps learners develop a key list of takeaways for their message

  - Exercises and hones learners' self-expression and articulation skills

  - Teaches learners that fully understanding their own intended message is the first step to getting others to understand it

## Medium

With an understanding of the content and the purpose as the foundation, students can then identify the following two additional components to consider the medium and build on the message.

- **Delivering:** Similar to solution fluency's deliver phase, delivering within the medium aspect of the leverage phase is about creating and implementing a final media project, using the medium to communicate the message with the audience within the predetermined constraints and success criteria—

- Contrasts and compares choices to help learners determine the perfect medium to deliver their message
- Helps learners develop a key list of takeaways for their message
- Exercises and hones learners' self-expression and articulation skills
- Teaches learners that fully understanding their own intended message is the first step to getting others to understand it

- **Reviewing:** Reviewing involves critical reflection and evaluation of the final product and production process against success criteria, making refinements if necessary—

  - Leads learners to see that the same information can be presented and interpreted in different ways
  - Develops learners' verbal and nonverbal communication skills
  - Gives learners a deeper understanding of the human psyche through knowing how people react to the same input in different ways
  - Helps learners come to respect others' opinions

# Media Fluency in Schools

Following are exemplars of inquiry- and project-based lessons that cultivate media fluency. We've provided samples that cover a variety of grade levels and subjects to ensure all readers have access to relevant, applicable examples. Readers can find the full lessons as well as the activities and assessment resources on the Solution Fluency Activity Planner (https://solutionfluency.com). See the extensive rubrics at the end of this chapter (figures 6.1–6.2, pages 96–102) for tools to facilitate assessment of these and other media fluency lessons.

## Mathematics Models (Primary School)

**Essential question:** What kind of visual representation can you use to illustrate an understanding of geometry?

**Subjects:** Mathematics, technology, art, design, language arts

**Scenario:** Exploring geometry is a fascinating adventure that can be visually exciting for any student. How? Well, why not answer that question yourself using mathematics and creativity combined?

Create a digital flipbook or other sort of lesson guide that teaches your favorite geometry lesson. Apply the principles of geometry and creative design together into a unique instructional experience. Think what would make a lesson exciting for you, both visually and from a teaching standpoint, and recreate it in your own way!

## Faraway Friends (Primary School)

**Essential question:** How can you combine your knowledge of mathematics, art, and design to help resolve a societal conflict?

**Subjects:** Social studies, design, science, media development, technology, language arts

**Scenario:** Amazing things are happening! Some visitors from another planet are assimilating with our culture, and advertising is focused around their own ideas and principles. But some people are against them, and fear the worst. You know them to be a peaceful and helpful race of beings. What kind of ad can you create to persuade the public that the visitors are our friends and allies?

Use a knowledge of the most persuasive media ads you've seen to design a supportive ad for our new extraterrestrial friends. Show the qualities about them that make them perfect partners in a mutually beneficial sharing of the beautiful planet Earth!

## Looking Back (Middle School)

**Essential question:** How does cause and effect relate to a chronological retelling of historical events?

**Subjects:** History, language arts, film studies, media development

**Scenario:** The historical films we enjoy would not be possible without cause and effect, and an understanding of chronological events in history. How would you write a treatment for your own historical epic?

You and your classmates are a team of historical investigators who are putting together a treatment for a major historical narrative film. Your treatment must address producers who could potentially buy the rights to your idea. Make sure you have crafted an entertaining fact-based idea that will grab their attention, and be as persuasive as you can. Show them you can make history exciting!

## Game Builders (Middle School)

**Essential question:** How would you use plot, character, and story outlining to build games?

**Subjects:** Language arts, design, art, technology

**Scenario:** A major video game producer has invited local kids to enter a contest where they design characters and a plot line for a video game. The contest is based on the theme of ordinary kids in extraordinary worlds.

Get ready to develop and produce an idea for a video game that features yourselves as the characters. The focus is all about plot, character development, and conflict. Create obstacles, challenges, and rewards, and fashion unique villains and opponents. Develop the elements of storytelling in a unique and thrilling video game!

## Mock Doc (High School)

Lessons that cultivate multiple fluencies appear in each applicable fluency.

**Essential question:** What goes on behind the scenes when making a documentary about an important topic?

**Subjects:** Language arts, design, media, technology, filmmaking

**Scenario:** Documentaries demonstrate an intimate knowledge about a particular subject, something that the creator cares very deeply about. Think about the documentaries you've seen on TV that you really enjoyed. What about them gave you that reaction?

Working in groups, pick a topic of interest to yourselves and create a full-fledged documentary on this amazing subject. Demonstrate your expertise about the steps involved in research and production, and get to know more about how documentaries are designed to be both informative and compelling!

## Selling an Idea (High School)

**Essential question:** How are the characteristics of advertisement used to shape our thinking?

**Subjects:** Language arts, media development, technology, art, marketing

**Scenario:** Every idea needs a kick start, and in today's world, ideas become great because of digital media. We have the power to develop, publish, and share them with wider and more diverse markets than we ever could have imagined. What's the idea you want to share?

You have a brand-new product you want to advertise, so figure out the best way to sell your idea. It will be advertised in a commercial that will appear on video-sharing sites, blogs, TVs, and cell phones globally. Your ad must have a central theme that complements the product. Be creative and eye-catching but not overwhelming. Create an ad that drives your product into high demand everywhere!

# Rubrics for Media Fluency

We provide the following rubrics as examples for evaluating student performance on items that contribute to media fluency, including descriptions of what student performance or work products might look like at each phase of the essential fluencies framework.

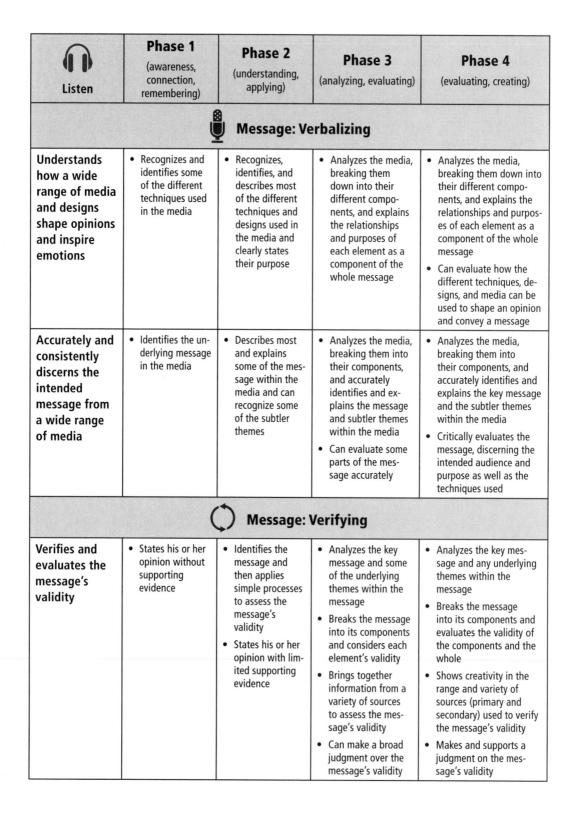

| Listen | Phase 1 (awareness, connection, remembering) | Phase 2 (understanding, applying) | Phase 3 (analyzing, evaluating) | Phase 4 (evaluating, creating) |
|---|---|---|---|---|
| **Message: Verbalizing** | | | | |
| **Understands how a wide range of media and designs shape opinions and inspire emotions** | • Recognizes and identifies some of the different techniques used in the media | • Recognizes, identifies, and describes most of the different techniques and designs used in the media and clearly states their purpose | • Analyzes the media, breaking them down into their different components, and explains the relationships and purposes of each element as a component of the whole message | • Analyzes the media, breaking them down into their different components, and explains the relationships and purposes of each element as a component of the whole message<br>• Can evaluate how the different techniques, designs, and media can be used to shape an opinion and convey a message |
| **Accurately and consistently discerns the intended message from a wide range of media** | • Identifies the underlying message in the media | • Describes most and explains some of the message within the media and can recognize some of the subtler themes | • Analyzes the media, breaking them into their components, and accurately identifies and explains the message and subtler themes within the media<br>• Can evaluate some parts of the message accurately | • Analyzes the media, breaking them into their components, and accurately identifies and explains the key message and the subtler themes within the media<br>• Critically evaluates the message, discerning the intended audience and purpose as well as the techniques used |
| **Message: Verifying** | | | | |
| **Verifies and evaluates the message's validity** | • States his or her opinion without supporting evidence | • Identifies the message and then applies simple processes to assess the message's validity<br>• States his or her opinion with limited supporting evidence | • Analyzes the key message and some of the underlying themes within the message<br>• Breaks the message into its components and considers each element's validity<br>• Brings together information from a variety of sources to assess the message's validity<br>• Can make a broad judgment over the message's validity | • Analyzes the key message and any underlying themes within the message<br>• Breaks the message into its components and evaluates the validity of the components and the whole<br>• Shows creativity in the range and variety of sources (primary and secondary) used to verify the message's validity<br>• Makes and supports a judgment on the message's validity |

| Listen | Phase 1 (awareness, connection, remembering) | Phase 2 (understanding, applying) | Phase 3 (analyzing, evaluating) | Phase 4 (evaluating, creating) |
|---|---|---|---|---|
| **Medium: Evaluating Form** | | | | |
| **Evaluates form** | • Shows an awareness of some of the guiding rules and principles for the medium | • Describes the product in terms of prominence, position, and proportion and considers some of the guiding principles and rules of each medium | • Considers the position, prominence, and proportion of most of the elements and considers their impact on and enhancement of the message<br>• Analyzes the product, breaking it into its components to examine the effectiveness of the form<br>• Considers most of the guiding principles and rules to present some evaluative comments | • Considers the position, prominence, and proportion of elements and the impact and enhancement each has on the message<br>• Analyzes the product, breaking it into its components to examine and then evaluate all or most of the elements for effectiveness<br>• Considers the guiding principles and rules of each medium to present a critical evaluation and judgment |
| **Medium: Evaluating Flow** | | | | |
| **Evaluates motion and momentum** | • Identifies some of the areas of flow within the message | • Describes or explains the flow in different aspects of the message and considers some of the critical aspects—pace, volume, motion, time, and so on | • Analyzes the flow of the message<br>• Breaks the message into suitable components and considers the effectiveness of some of the elements in terms of time, pace, volume, or motion when analyzing<br>• Offers some limited evaluation | • Analyzes the flow of the message<br>• Breaks the message into suitable components and considers the effectiveness of the elements in terms of time, pace, volume, and motion when analyzing<br>• Evaluates the effectiveness of the use of the different elements of flow and offers a critical supported judgment |
| **Evaluates harmony and balance** | • Struggles to describe the message in terms of harmony or balance | • Describes or explains the balance and harmony of the message | • Analyzes the messages with consideration of the harmony and balance of the message<br>• Links harmony and balance to the purpose of the message<br>• Offers limited evaluation | • Analyzes the messages with detailed consideration of the harmony and balance of the message<br>• Identifies the relationship and linkage between the elements of the message<br>• Relates the harmony and balance to the purpose of the message and then evaluates the success of the implementation of these aspects |

**Figure 6.1: Media fluency assessment rubric—Listen.** continued →

| Listen | Phase 1 (awareness, connection, remembering) | Phase 2 (understanding, applying) | Phase 3 (analyzing, evaluating) | Phase 4 (evaluating, creating) |
|---|---|---|---|---|
| **Medium: Evaluating Alignment** | | | | |
| **Discerns alignment in the application of media to a message and purpose in a variety of formats** | • Identifies some of the elements of the message | • Examines the message and describes or explains most of the different components of the message | • Examines the message and analyzes the different components of the medium, audience, and message<br>• Offers some evaluation of these elements and develops a judgment of the solution or product's success | • Critically examines the message, analyzing the different components of the medium, audience, and message itself<br>• Critically evaluates these elements and develops a focused and insightful judgment of the solution or product's success |

*Visit **go.SolutionTree.com/assessment** for a free reproducible version of this figure.*

| Leverage | Phase 1 (awareness, connection, remembering) | Phase 2 (understanding, applying) | Phase 3 (analyzing, evaluating) | Phase 4 (evaluating, creating) |
|---|---|---|---|---|
| **Message: Considering Audience** | | | | |
| **Identifies the audience and considers its needs, preferences, and motivations** | • Identifies the target audience for the message | • Identifies the target audience for the message<br>• Describes or explains some of the elements that need to be included in the message to suit the audience or demographic | • Identifies the target audience for the message<br>• Analyzes the message, medium, and form for the requirements and preferences of the audience or demographic<br>• Identifies some of the areas, aspects, or elements needed for this audience or demographic based on the analysis<br>• Offers some limited evaluation of the success for the target audience | • Identifies the target audience for the message<br>• Analyzes the message, medium, and form for the requirements and preferences of the audience or demographic<br>• Identifies critical areas, aspects, or elements needed for this audience or demographic based on the analysis<br>• Offers a supported and thoughtful judgment about the suitability of the message for the audience |
| **Message: Considering Outcome** | | | | |
| **Defines the purpose of a communication and considers how the form of a message influences the outcome** | • Defines the purpose or outcome of the product | • Determines the outcome to achieve<br>• Describes or explains the outcome or purpose of the message with some reference to the audience and available media<br>• Partly develops success criteria to measure the success of the product | • Determines the outcome to achieve<br>• Analyzes the outcome or purpose of the message, considering the target audience and available media<br>• Makes a limited evaluation of the suitability of the audience's outcome or purpose and uses this outcome to develop some of the success criteria and a suitable product | • Determines the outcome to achieve<br>• Analyzes the outcome or purpose of the message, considering the target audience and available media<br>• Analyzes and evaluates the audience's outcome or purpose for suitability and alignment and uses this outcome to develop success criteria and a suitable effective product |

**Figure 6.2: Media fluency assessment rubric—Leverage.** continued →

| Leverage | Phase 1 (awareness, connection, remembering) | Phase 2 (understanding, applying) | Phase 3 (analyzing, evaluating) | Phase 4 (evaluating, creating) |
|---|---|---|---|---|
| **Message: Considering Content** | | | | |
| **Provides content for conveying the message** | • States the outcome or purpose of the message<br>• States some of the content that is required for the message | • Describes the outcome or purpose of the message<br>• Describes the content that is required to convey the message | • Analyzes the outcome or purpose of the message<br>• Considers the content required to successfully convey the message with reference to the desired outcome and purpose<br>• Refines the content as required | • Analyzes and evaluates the outcome or purpose of the message<br>• Considers the content required to successfully convey the message, evaluating it against the outcome and purpose and refining the content as required |
| **Designs a product for conveying the message** | • Attempts to develop a plan | • Develops a design that will meet some of the success criteria<br>• Makes some refinements to the product | • Develops a design based on the requirements of the audience and the purpose<br>• Analyzes the design against the success criteria and refines it as needed | • Develops a suitable design based on the requirements of the audience and the purpose of the product<br>• Evaluates the design against the success criteria<br>• Refines the design to meet the requirements of the success criteria, purpose, and audience as required |
| **Uses feasible method for conveying content** | • Identifies some of the aspects of feasibility that may need consideration | • Describes different elements of feasibility and how they relate to his or her product | • Analyzes the task in terms of feasibility<br>• Offers limited evaluation of the suitability of the product<br>• Refines the design, purpose, or success criteria as required | • Analyzes the task in terms of feasibility and then evaluates the suitability of the product based on his or her consideration of feasibility<br>• Refines the design, purpose, or success criteria as required and justifies the changes |

| Leverage | Phase 1 (awareness, connection, remembering) | Phase 2 (understanding, applying) | Phase 3 (analyzing, evaluating) | Phase 4 (evaluating, creating) |
|---|---|---|---|---|
| **Medium: Delivering** | | | | |
| (For detailed consideration of this aspect, please use Solution Fluency. See chapter 3.) | | | | |
| **Produces the product consistently with the outcome** | • Develops a product that is partly functional or only partly complete, addresses some of the success criteria, and is partially suitable for the audience or purpose | • Develops a product that is mostly consistent with the outcome, meets some success criteria, and is functional | • Develops a product that is suitable for the purpose and audience, is consistent with the outcome, meets most of the success criteria, and is functional<br>• Can identify changes from the original plan, process, or design and justify some of them | • Develops a product that is suitable for the purpose and audience, is consistent with the outcome, meets the success criteria, is fully functional, and shows care and attention to detail<br>• Fully justifies any changes from the original plan, process, or design |
| **Produces the product within the constraints and success criteria** | • Struggles to remain within the process constraints<br>• Has some awareness of the limitations, restrictions, and so on | • Applies the criteria and generally remains within the process constraints<br>• States the goals, outcomes, and limitations of the process and product | • Consistently analyzes and breaks down the process or product and compares against the success criteria<br>• Offers some limited evaluation and sometimes revises the design, success criteria, and plan<br>• Can partly justify changes and modifications | • Consistently analyzes and evaluates the process and product against the success criteria to ensure accuracy<br>• Evaluates and revises the design, success criteria, and plan as required<br>• Justifies the changes and modifications as required<br>• Informs stakeholders of substantial changes if required |
| **Medium: Reviewing** | | | | |
| **Develops suitable success criteria** | • Identifies some of the success criteria | • Describes some of the success criteria for the product or solution | • Applies the purpose, requirements of the audience, and design elements to developed criteria to evaluate the product or solution | • Applies the purpose, requirements of the audience, and design elements to developed suitable criteria to evaluate the success of the product or solution<br>• Evaluates the criteria, considering all critical aspects |

continued →

| Leverage | Phase 1 (awareness, connection, remembering) | Phase 2 (understanding, applying) | Phase 3 (analyzing, evaluating) | Phase 4 (evaluating, creating) |
|---|---|---|---|---|
| **Uses success criteria to evaluate the product and identify completion of the project** | • Identifies some of the elements that match the success criteria | • Matches success criteria to the elements of the product<br>• Can make some relevant and appropriate refinements | • Applies the success criteria to evaluate the solution<br>• Makes limited or unsupported judgments of the success of the product and refines it | • Accurately applies the criteria to evaluate the solution and make judgments of the success of the product<br>• Refines the product based on the application of the success criteria, or suggests future developments or process refinements for further iterations or new processes |

*Visit **go.SolutionTree.com/assessment** for a free reproducible version of this figure.*

As more and more communication is happening in media beyond text and speech, the ability to decode messages and to construct our own effective communications is more essential than ever. Media fluency can be used as a structured way to both break down media as a consumer and develop media as a creator, making us more effective communicators in a digital world.

# Guiding Questions

Before moving to the next chapter, answer the following questions as an individual or with your school team.

1. Why is it just as important for us to know why we produce messages in media as it is for us to know how to do it?

2. In what ways have we become a visual society, and why is this important to how we approach school projects?

3. Why is it just as important for our students to be able to communicate as proficiently with multiple media formats as they do with speech and text?

4. How are you and your students using media fluency in your classroom? If you are not, how do you think you would begin with the current levels of technology available to you?

# chapter 7

# Collaboration Fluency

Our present and future classrooms and workforces are built on global virtual communication. When it comes to both learning and play, today's digital native students possess a natural urge to work in groups and teams. It's not uncommon to see them teaming up on school projects or video game sessions with several collaborators at one time. Many of these team members live far away from each other. Collaborating with others is automatic and ubiquitous among our youth. This aspect of the digital native student's nature is what collaboration fluency addresses. Collaboration fluency refers to teams whose working proficiency has reached the mechanical ability to work cooperatively with virtual and real partners in online environments to create original digital products. The 5Es of collaboration fluency are: (1) establish, (2) envision, (3) engineer, (4) execute, and (5) examine. In this chapter, we will describe these aspects, note some skills each helps to cultivate, and list potential benefits that result from developing those skills. We then provide rubrics for measuring items that students require to be successful with the aspects of collaboration fluency.

## Establish

Building anything, including great collaborative teams, requires a solid foundation. Learners should ask themselves what challenge they and their dream team face, who the best people are to help them, and where they are in terms of assembling the group they want.

Addressing this includes establishing group members, roles and responsibilities, norms, scope of the project, information needs, and leaders, and committing them all to a group contract. The skills that students develop in the establish stage, and the beneficial opportunities and possibilities that utilizing each creates, include the following.

- Assembling the group:
  - Develops leadership and organizational abilities

- Hones interpersonal skills as learners interact with possible candidates and learn their strengths and weaknesses
- Lets learners move forward in confidence knowing that the group has come together for a common goal

- Determining areas of expertise:
  - Helps learners narrow down their search for filling individual roles
  - Lets learners match an individual's strengths to a particular team role
  - Allows learners to get a sense of who is willing and able to learn new skills
  - Uncovers surprising things about learners' peers that they may not have known before

- Specifying individual roles and responsibilities:
  - Identifies personal responsibilities as well as responsibilities to the rest of the team
  - Develops group organizational skills among the team members
  - Establishes a valuable sense of accountability for each team member

- Establishing communication practices:
  - Helps learners establish the communication norms that are the most practical and agreeable for all team members
  - Ensures a team's best performance and progress
  - Establishes favorable accountability guidelines for team communications
  - Allows for effective and open communication within the team

- Framing the challenge:
  - Leads learners to hear unique opinions and perspectives from others
  - Motivates the team to think and to develop the next steps as a cohesive unit
  - Gives the team a clear picture of what it needs to accomplish

- Outlining project and performance expectations:
  - Reinforces accountability and unity in the team
  - Gives team members a clear vision and outcomes to strive for
  - Clarifies individual expectations for all team members
  - Allows learners to establish realistic time lines for personal and team goals and outcomes

# Envision

At this stage the group visualizes, defines, and examines the purpose, issue, challenge, preferred solution, or goal. It also develops an agreement about the outcome and the criteria for evaluating it. The skills that students develop in the envision stage, and the beneficial opportunities and possibilities that utilizing each creates, include the following.

- Defining the current problem or situation:
  - Informs team members of the problem they are collectively solving
  - Gives the problem the proper context for the whole group
  - Invites the group to share insights about collective goals and expectations
- Visualizing a desired future:
  - Ensures that the team works toward a unified goal
  - Inspires and encourages the team to think about possibilities without limits
  - Discovers that the impossible may actually be possible sometimes
  - Encourages brainstorming activities that hone communication skills
- Specifying information needs:
  - Promotes critical thinking and deep understanding of learners' creative wishes through asking good questions
  - Makes the information gathering process move quickly through an organized team approach
  - Gives learners a better understanding of the nature of the problem
- Identifying all available information:
  - Gives learners a starting point for organizing and utilizing data
  - Allows learners to discern what information is missing and what they don't need
  - Indicates that learners may be closer to formulating a solution than they originally thought
- Developing criteria for evaluating the outcome:
  - Helps learners identify and verbalize the desired outcome
  - Allows the team to work together to decide how it will measure success once it creates a solution
  - Encourages more focus on generating the best solution possible
  - Encourages a very thorough understanding of the problem

# Engineer

Engineering a workable plan means breaking out all the necessary steps to get learners from where they are to where they want to be. The team collaboratively works backward from the desired end point to develop the plan. The skills that students develop in the engineer stage, and the beneficial opportunities and possibilities that utilizing each creates, include the following.

- Creating the actual plan:
    - Guides the work and allows learners to check, discuss, and re-evaluate it
    - Allows a team to check off milestones, motivating team members and providing a sense of accomplishment
    - Ensures consistent communication and accountability among team members through set guidelines
    - Allows learners to plan ahead for the unexpected and unforeseen
- Delegating responsibilities efficiently:
    - Lets learners call on individual strengths among the team members
    - Demonstrates the efficacy of matching the person to the role, rather than matching the role to a person who may not be suitable
    - Divides the work fairly among the team members
    - Allows the team to achieve more overall
    - Allows team members to develop their skills and contribute to the solution in meaningful ways
    - Reinforces how team members rely on each other to accomplish goals

# Execute

In this stage, learners put the plan into action, focusing on the development of a tangible, viable solution or product that best uses the team members' individual strengths. The skills that students develop in the execute stage, and the beneficial opportunities and possibilities that utilizing each creates, include the following.

- Identifying the best format for presenting solutions:
    - Allows learners to become familiar with different multimedia formats
    - Helps you learn which media are best for certain environments and audiences using media fluency skills
    - Encourages the team to consider its audience's needs and expectations for its presentation

- Allows the group to explore how it can use different media formats to communicate a message

- Guides the team members toward considering what they really want to accomplish with any message they want to share

- Using the format to convey the solution:

  - Engages one's audience and helps it retain the knowledge the team of learners delivers

  - Helps the team work together to find creative ways to deliver the solution

  - Connects the team's ideas with real-world events and experiences

  - Sparks lively discussions about the solution among the team and the audience

  - Helps the team share opinions with others in a constructive manner

# Examine

Examine involves looking back at the process and determining whether the challenge was met and the goal achieved, identifying areas of improvement, recognizing contributions, and giving constructive feedback. The skills that students develop in the examine stage, and the beneficial opportunities and possibilities that utilizing each creates, include the following.

- Reconsidering each stage of the process:

  - Lets learners determine as a group where they were most unified in their efforts, and also where there were disconnects

  - Allows learners to see what they could have done more efficiently

  - Encourages a proactive review of the process

  - Promotes constructive team evaluations and assessments

- Reflecting critically on the product or process:

  - Develops the team's collaborative communication skills

  - Sets the tone for a more lengthy discussion about how the team used collaboration fluency's 5Es

  - Lets the team consider what worked well and what it could have done better

  - Allows learners to share opinions and viewpoints constructively

- Acting on reflections:

  - Provides an opportunity for the team to move forward in a positive way

  - Gives every team member a chance to apply new skills and knowledge

- Reinforces a sense of accountability and responsibility across the team
- Continues the development of the entire team's collaborative and inter-personal skills
  - Internalizing and using new learning:
    - Makes the learning stick—the more learners practice this process, the more automatic or fluent it becomes
    - Makes problem solving easier with an internalized process
    - Presents problems as opportunities for greater learning
    - Better prepares the team to handle future challenges
  - Transferring learning to new or different situations:
    - Hones the team's ability to apply the information to current and future challenges in practical ways
    - Gives the team a chance to share its newfound wisdom to help others in new situations
    - Uncovers ways to improve or revise a product
    - Allows learners to revisit the 5E stages and gain new insights
  - Recognizing team members' contributions:
    - Facilitates the well-being of any cohesive team
    - Gives team members a chance to get individual recognition for their work and time
    - Lets the team members support each other and provide their peers with positive reinforcement
    - Conveys appreciation of extra work and effort

# Collaboration Fluency in Schools

Following are exemplars of inquiry- and project-based lessons that cultivate collaboration fluency. We've provided samples that cover a variety of grade levels and subjects to ensure all readers have access to relevant, applicable examples. Readers can find the full lessons as well as the activities and assessment resources on the Solution Fluency Activity Planner (https://solutionfluency.com). See the extensive rubrics at the end of this chapter (figures 7.1–7.5, pages 111–117) for tools to facilitate assessment of these and other collaboration fluency lessons.

## *Citizenship Day (Primary School)*

**Essential question:** What can you do to help make people aware of online responsibility?

**Subjects:** Language arts, art, design, mathematics, science

**Scenario:** You and your friends want to show others how important it is that we learn to treat each other (and ourselves) with respect in our new digital environments. This is *digital citizenship*.

Work together to find out the practices of good digital citizenship, and create unique class participation games that teach people about digital citizenship. Then, invite other students and teachers—and even parents—to play your games and learn about digital citizenship in a class activity day!

## Tour Guide (Primary School)

**Essential question:** How can you use mapping technologies to attract tourists to a region?

**Subjects:** Social studies, design, geography, language arts, technology

**Scenario:** Your local chamber of commerce wants to attract tourists to your area in order to boost the economy. Why not create a guided tour of your town, city, or local area? Map absolute coordinates for each stop, write descriptions of each landmark, and use Google Earth to record the tour for prospective tourists.

Record a virtual tour on Google Earth that can be posted onto a website. Give your tour three to five locations to stop at including at least two local geographic landmarks (mountains, rivers, and so on) and one historical point of interest. Use Google Earth's voice-over narrative function (www.google.com/earth/outreach/tutorials/kmltours .html) to guide the viewers through your amazing tour!

## Atomic Rock (Middle School)

**Essential question:** How can we use performing arts to teach others the scientific properties of matter?

**Subjects:** Science, music, digital media, language arts, theater

**Scenario:** A local TV network wants science classes in your grade to work together to create a musical segment for its show. The songs they are looking for must be entertaining, and they need to provide an informative science lesson for children about the properties of matter. Put on your lab coats, grab your guitars, and get rocking!

Science unites with music in this fun lesson that lets you teach and learn about the properties of matter by using original songs as your teaching method! Combine scientific research with your love of music to instruct younger students on the properties of matter in creative and entertaining original songs. Make science rock!

## Party Planners (Middle School)

Lessons that cultivate multiple fluencies appear in each applicable fluency.

**Essential question:** How do party planners use proportional reasoning to determine costs and quantities of refreshments for guests?

**Subjects:** Mathematics, language arts, technology, design, economics

**Scenario:** Everybody loves a party! There is a lot of work involved to make a party event successful. It's design, it's mathematics, it's economics—and nobody throws a party like you and your friends!

Plan the ultimate party by creating the menu from actual recipes, and determine the quantities of food for each recipe that you'll need for 175 guests. Use a ratio relationship to adjust the amounts given in the recipe and include a table showing the original amounts next to the adjusted amounts. Then, plan and design the party space, and figure out the costs for supplies, and how you can stretch your budget while still making the event memorable!

## The Greenway (High School)

**Essential question:** How do greenways and green transportation routes improve the quality of the environment in large cities?

**Subjects:** Social studies, design, urban planning, technology, sustainability, digital media

**Scenario:** It's time for you to start thinking green! Work in groups to design and present ideas for a green transportation corridor in your city. Become inspired by actual urban-planning procedures and follow examples of eco-friendly initiatives other cities put in place.

As a team, research a suitable transportation corridor or other location that could accommodate a pedestrian walkway, bicycle lane, or commuter trail or pathway. Design the walkway or bicycle lane with aesthetics in mind, and make sure it is wide enough to accommodate two directions of traffic. Use natural elements such as grass, trees, or other foliage to make your greenway something your city can be proud of!

## Irrational Land (High School)

**Essential question:** How can irrational numbers be used in the creation of an imaginary landscape?

**Subjects:** Mathematics, design, technology, visual arts, digital media, language arts

**Scenario:** In an imaginary landscape, everything can change. As virtual reality designers, you and your team have decided to create a fictitious place called Irrational

Land where all measurement is done using irrational numbers. Why? Because Hollywood has its eye on you!

Create a unique three-dimensional model for a virtual reality landscape where all measurement is done using irrational numbers. Develop tools that use irrational numbers to measure places, structures, and objects in this imaginary landscape. Then deliver a five-minute pitch to persuade a film director to use your landscape as the location in an upcoming fantasy film!

# Rubrics for Collaboration Fluency

We provide the following rubrics as examples for evaluating student performance on items that contribute to collaboration fluency, including descriptions of what student performance or work products might look like at each phase of the essential fluencies framework.

| Establish | Phase 1 (awareness, connection, remembering) | Phase 2 (understanding, applying) | Phase 3 (analyzing, evaluating) | Phase 4 (evaluating, creating) |
|---|---|---|---|---|
| Effectively participates as a team member and knows his or her own capacities for filling different team roles | • Shows little awareness of his or her own abilities and weaknesses<br>• Has a marked preference for his or her role in the team, and will not willingly change from it<br>• Is sometimes supportive of others and occasionally makes effective contributions | • Shows some awareness of his or her own abilities and weaknesses<br>• Shows ability to act in different roles in the team, but has a marked preference for one role<br>• Can be supportive of others and will sometimes make effective contributions<br>• Will sometimes offer critique that is appropriate | • Demonstrates a level of self-awareness with some understanding of his or her own abilities and weaknesses<br>• Shows ability to act in the different team roles, but has a preference for one role<br>• Can be supportive when others have the leadership role and often makes effective contributions<br>• Is predominantly supportive and encouraging and can offer appropriate critique<br>• When in a leadership role, shows openness to advice and suggestions and often supports an inclusive decision-making model | • Demonstrates a high level of self-awareness<br>• Has a realistic understanding of his or her own abilities and weaknesses<br>• Moves easily between different team roles<br>• Shows support when others have the leadership role, and makes effective contributions<br>• Remains supportive and encouraging, providing focused and appropriate critique when required<br>• In a leadership role, shows openness to advice and suggestions and can fully support an inclusive decision-making model |

**Figure 7.1: Collaboration fluency assessment rubric—Establish.**

continued →

| Establish | Phase 1 (awareness, connection, remembering) | Phase 2 (understanding, applying) | Phase 3 (analyzing, evaluating) | Phase 4 (evaluating, creating) |
|---|---|---|---|---|
| **Demonstrates proficiency in managing personal relationships** | • Shows little awareness of the others within the team<br>• Struggles to identify his or her teammates' strengths and weaknesses<br>• Struggles to be culturally aware and supportive of others' differences | • Shows some awareness of the others within the team<br>• Identifies his or her teammates' strengths and weaknesses and can apply this understanding to use his or her teammates' abilities<br>• Mostly supportive of his or her peers and can sometimes offer appropriate critique<br>• Sometimes manages conflict in a mature, nonjudgmental manner<br>• Shows an awareness of cultural differences, frequently applying general guidelines when interacting with his or her peers<br>• Will sometimes not tolerate inappropriate behavior and will occasionally act to deal with it | • Demonstrates an awareness of the others within the team<br>• Can identify and consider his or her teammates' strengths and weaknesses and can often effectively use their strengths<br>• Is supportive of his or her peers overall, frequently offering critique that is appropriate and task centered<br>• Often manages conflict in a mature, nonjudgmental manner<br>• Shows an awareness of cultural differences and sometimes uses these as guidelines for interactions<br>• Will not tolerate inappropriate behavior and will frequently act to deal with it | • Demonstrates a broad and realistic awareness of the others within the team<br>• Evaluates his or her team members' strengths and weaknesses and effectively uses their strengths<br>• Is supportive of his or her peers, offering critique that is appropriate, task centered, and formative, enabling his or her peers to improve and develop<br>• Manages conflict in a mature, nonjudgmental manner<br>• Demonstrates awareness of cultural differences and uses them as guidelines for interactions<br>• Will not tolerate inappropriate behavior and will act appropriately and ethically to deal with it |
| **Develops a group contract** | • Develops a group contract predominantly focused on a common goal or objective | • Develops a group contract that establishes the expected behaviors for the group and that predominantly focuses on a common goal or objective | • Develops a group contract that establishes the expected behaviors for the group, providing some guidelines for interaction and conflict resolution, and that focuses on a common goal or objective | • Develops a clearly defined group contract that clearly establishes the expected behaviors for the group, providing guidelines for appropriate interaction and conflict resolution, that allows for individuality while supporting a common goal or objective, and that encompasses rather than excludes |

*Visit **go.SolutionTree.com/assessment** for a free reproducible version of this figure.*

| ◉ Envision | Phase 1 (awareness, connection, remembering) | Phase 2 (understanding, applying) | Phase 3 (analyzing, evaluating) | Phase 4 (evaluating, creating) |
|---|---|---|---|---|
| **Interacts with others to generate ideas and develop products** | • Defines the task<br>• Listens to others' input and occasionally combines his or her own and peers' concepts to produce an understanding of the task, problem, or issue | • Defines and explains the task to the team or group<br>• Frequently listens to others' input and combines his or her own and peers' concepts to produce an understanding of the task, problem, or issue<br>• Attempts to ensure team members contribute | • Defines and explains the task, including its parts, to the team or group<br>• Listens to others' input and combines his or her own and peers' concepts to produce an understanding of the task, problem, or issue<br>• Frequently uses techniques and approaches to ensure team members contribute | • Clearly defines and articulately explains the task, its parts, and their implications to the team or group<br>• Listens to others' input and effectively combines his or her own and peers' concepts into an inclusive understanding of the task, problem, or issue<br>• Uses suitable techniques and approaches to ensure all team members contribute<br>• Uses effective probing questions to develop a realistic understanding of the task by challenging assumptions, prior knowledge, and bias |
| **Uses appropriate interpersonal skills within a variety of media and social contexts** | • Has some awareness of the features of the different media he or she operates in and can sometimes use them effectively | • Has an awareness of the features of the different media he or she operates in and can use them effectively | • Has an awareness of the strengths and limitations of the different media he or she operates in<br>• Breaks down the different features of the media and can use them effectively<br>• Can sometimes suggest alternative approaches, processes, or mechanisms | • Has detailed awareness of the strengths and limitations of the different media he or she operates in<br>• Evaluates strengths and limitations and is able to leverage the best aspect of the medium and take into account its limitations when interacting with his or her peers<br>• Suggests alternative approaches, processes, or mechanisms when required |

**Figure 7.2: Collaboration fluency assessment rubric—Envision.**

continued →

| Envision | Phase 1 (awareness, connection, remembering) | Phase 2 (understanding, applying) | Phase 3 (analyzing, evaluating) | Phase 4 (evaluating, creating) |
|---|---|---|---|---|
| Understands the creative process through collaboration, the exchange of ideas, and building on the achievements of others | • Identifies the stage of development the group is in<br>• Can sometimes refocus him- or herself on the task at hand<br>• Is occasionally supportive of his or her peers | • Shows some understanding of the different stages of group formation<br>• Identifies the stage of development the group is in<br>• Refocuses the group on the task at hand<br>• Is frequently supportive of his or her peers | • Shows understanding of the different stages of group formation<br>• Shows ability to undertake limited evaluation of the stage the group is in<br>• Analyzes the progress of the group and can sometimes refocus the group on the task<br>• Is often supportive and inclusive | • Shows detailed understanding of the different stages of group formation<br>• Evaluates the stage that the group as a whole or individual participants are in and adapts interactions accordingly<br>• Evaluates the progress of the individual or the group and can effectively refocus the group or individuals on the task as required<br>• Is supportive and inclusive at all times |

*Visit **go.SolutionTree.com/assessment** for a free reproducible version of this figure.*

| ![Engineer] Engineer | Phase 1 (awareness, connection, remembering) | Phase 2 (understanding, applying) | Phase 3 (analyzing, evaluating) | Phase 4 (evaluating, creating) |
|---|---|---|---|---|
| **Aligns work to goals and vision** | • Sometimes applies the defined process<br>• Is sometimes cooperative and collaborative<br>• Struggles to be receptive to feedback and critique | • Applies a process that will see most of the group's goals and objectives achieved<br>• Is often cooperative and collaborative<br>• Is generally receptive to feedback and can sometimes offer appropriate critique | • Designs a process that will see most of the group's goals and objectives achieved and that will use some of the group members' strengths<br>• Is frequently cooperative and collaborative, often incorporating suggestions and criticism from peers to improve the process<br>• Frequently offers appropriate, task-focused critique | • Designs a process that will see the group's goals and objectives achieved and that is efficient, using the group members' strengths appropriately<br>• Is cooperative and collaborative, appropriately incorporating the suggestions and criticism from peers to improve the process<br>• Offers appropriate, task-focused critique |
| **Develops and implements an effective plan** | • Shows an awareness of the process and the current stage of development<br>• Sometimes describes problems | • Generally applies appropriate milestones and stages to the process<br>• Uses checkpoints to measure progress on the project<br>• Often describes problems and develops some solutions | • Creates a process that has appropriate milestones and stages<br>• Uses regular checkpoints to measure progress on the assigned tasks<br>• Defines each person's tasks within the process<br>• Discusses problems and develops suitable solutions | • Creates a process with clearly defined and appropriate milestones and stages<br>• Manages progress on the assigned tasks using regular checkpoints<br>• Clearly defines each person's roles and responsibilities within each element of the process<br>• Effectively articulates problems and develops suitable solutions in an inclusive manner |
| **Accesses resources** | • Identifies some of the resources for the task<br>• Often uses resources inefficiently, uneconomically, or wastefully | • Identifies most of the resources for the task and matches them with available resources | • Identifies the resources for the task and matches them with available resources<br>• Takes actions to source required resources, or puts some modifications in place to cope with the deficit | • Accurately identifies the required resources for the task and matches them with available resources<br>• Takes appropriate actions to source required resources, or puts modifications in place to cope with the deficit<br>• Uses resources efficiently, economically, and in a timely fashion |

*Visit **go.SolutionTree.com/assessment** for a free reproducible version of this figure.*

**Figure 7.3: Collaboration fluency assessment rubric—Engineer.**

| ⎈ Execute | Phase 1 (awareness, connection, remembering) | Phase 2 (understanding, applying) | Phase 3 (analyzing, evaluating) | Phase 4 (evaluating, creating) |
|---|---|---|---|---|
| **Works collaboratively toward a common, shared goal or objective** | • Sometimes works with peers to achieve the group's goals<br>• Is sometimes on task when working independently | • Works with peers collaboratively or individually to achieve the group's goals<br>• Measures individual group progress against the goals and objectives | • Works with peers collaboratively or individually to achieve the group's goals<br>• Analyzes individual or group progress against the goals and objectives and sometimes offers appropriate critique<br>• Is often inclusive with peers | • Works with peers collaboratively and economically or individually to achieve the group's goals<br>• Analyzes and evaluates individual or group progress against the goals and objectives and offers appropriate critique or undertakes suitable actions as required<br>• Is inclusive with peers |
| **Productively collaborates across networks using various technologies** | • Struggles to operate in a variety of different media | • Operates in a variety of different media | • Operates in a variety of different media, showing some understanding of their strengths and weaknesses | • Operates effectively and efficiently in a variety of different media, showing understanding of their strengths and weaknesses |

Visit **go.SolutionTree.com/assessment** *for a free reproducible version of this figure.*

**Figure 7.4: Collaboration fluency assessment rubric—Execute.**

| Examine | Phase 1 (awareness, connection, remembering) | Phase 2 (understanding, applying) | Phase 3 (analyzing, evaluating) | Phase 4 (evaluating, creating) |
|---|---|---|---|---|
| Revisits, reflects critically on, and revises the individual and group process and contribution at each stage | • Sometimes is able to reflect on progress against the overall objectives<br><br>• Struggles to accept feedback and seldom modifies actions or behaviors based on it | • Reflects on process and progress against the overall objectives<br><br>• Will sometimes offer useful reflections<br><br>• Often accepts feedback, sometimes modifying actions or behaviors based on it | • Reflects on the process, analyzing his or her own contribution and that of peers against the overall objectives<br><br>• Offers reflections that are task focused and appropriate<br><br>• Accepts feedback, sometimes modifying actions or behaviors based on it | • Reflects on the process, evaluating his or her own contribution and that of peers fairly<br><br>• Offers critical reflections that are task focused and appropriate, enabling growth and development of him- or herself or peers or refinement of processes and structures<br><br>• Accepts suitable and appropriate feedback, modifying tasks, actions, or behaviors based on this |
| Revisits, reflects critically on, and revises the planning and product at each stage | • Sometimes states the group's and his or her own individual progress against the milestones | • Describes the group's and his or her own individual progress against the milestones and often updates goals, objectives, processes, structures, and mechanisms | • Analyzes the group's and his or her own individual progress against the milestones and is able to update goals, objectives, processes, structures, and mechanisms as required | • Maintains suitable milestones and checkpoints and has a realistic evaluation of progress against these markers<br><br>• Adapts and refines goals, objectives, processes, structures, and mechanisms as required<br><br>• When required, takes suitable critical interactions to refocus the group or end the project |

*Visit **go.SolutionTree.com/assessment** for a free reproducible version of this figure.*

**Figure 7.5: Collaboration fluency assessment rubric—Examine.**

Collaboration has evolved from being in the same room to, in today's 24/7 wired world, reaching across the globe! It is essential that we all develop exceptional collaboration skills. The opportunity that exists now to work with others in structured ways will lead to globally developed solutions to our biggest global challenges.

# Guiding Questions

Before moving to the next chapter, answer the following questions as an individual or with your school team.

1.  What do you feel are the primary reasons why modern learners are naturally collaborative?

2. Why is having a shared vision so crucial to any team's success, and how does this apply to students in our classrooms?

3. Considering how technology has changed how we communicate, what are the advantages of being proficient at collaborating in both face-to-face and virtual environments?

4. Why is it important for team members to agree to a group contract? How would you go about introducing this idea to students for use in their own groups?

# chapter 8

# Global Digital Citizenship

Our level of global interconnectedness has been staggering since the World Wide Web was introduced into our lives. This interconnectedness allows us to see how collective or individual efforts can have a global effect. We can now see and track our actions on an international scale, measure our impact on the global environment, gauge our social and moral differences and similarities, rally together to inspire hope, and provide aid for countries, communities, or even individuals dealing with hardships and tragedies.

We have become very aware of our need to understand this continuous rapid change and forecast parameters of safety for our most vulnerable users. When we think about it, it makes sense to cultivate empowered individuals who are dutifully aware of their responsibility both for and with the power of the Internet for the lasting well-being of our global community.

This is a hallmark of what we call the *global digital citizen*: a conscientious, respectful, and compassionate individual who strives to establish a sense of global community in all his or her online and offline relationships, duties, and endeavors. The five unique aspects that define the global digital citizen are: (1) personal responsibility, (2) global citizenship, (3) digital citizenship, (4) altruistic service, and (5) environmental stewardship. In this chapter, we will describe these aspects, note some skills each helps to cultivate, and list potential benefits that result from developing those skills. We then provide rubrics for measuring items that students require to be successful with the aspects of global digital citizenship.

## Personal Responsibility

Personal responsibility shifts the responsibility for learning from the teacher toward the student in an effort to develop student accountability for lifelong learning. This fosters personal responsibility for financial matters, ethical and moral boundaries, personal health and fitness, and relationships of all kinds (Global Digital Citizen Foundation, 2015b).

Personal responsibility skills and processes, and the beneficial opportunities and possibilities that utilizing each creates, include the following.

- Taking responsibility for learning:
    - Develops the capacity and desire to learn independently
    - Encourages lifelong learning as a habit of mind
    - Creates a sense of pride and accomplishment
    - Adds to learners' capacity to be able to teach and learn from others
- Nurturing relationships of all kinds:
    - Encourages learners to learn proper ways to communicate
    - Fosters compassion and empathy, and helps learners grow personally
    - Gives learners an opportunity to learn things from other people
    - Helps learners respond to conflict with civility and constructive thinking
    - Helps learners begin to understand all the ways in which we are connected
- Maintaining physical, mental, and emotional health:
    - Contributes to inner balance and helps learners better manage everyday affairs
    - Increases learners' longevity and ability to enjoy life at any age
    - Helps diminish stress on the mind and body and make learners more resilient
    - Contributes to whole-being wellness and stability
- Managing financial matters:
    - Helps learners understand the responsibility that comes with wealth of any kind
    - Encourages lifelong smart financial management strategies
    - Shows learners the value of hard work and maintaining its rewards
- Developing ethical and moral standards:
    - Teaches the value of treating others with respect
    - Helps learners understand the fundamental differences between right and wrong, just and unjust, and moral and immoral
    - Provides learners with personal guidelines for living honest and charitable lives and setting an example for others
    - Contributes to our whole society's safety and well-being

# Global Citizenship

Twenty-first century technology and digital media have enabled communication, collaboration, dialogue, and debate among citizens of the world and across all levels of society. Global citizenship encourages students to therefore understand that we are not isolated—that we are all citizens of the world. Recognizing this leads to more awareness of the issues, traditions, religions, core values, and cultures of our fellow citizens and promotes tolerance and understanding, which are intertwined with acceptance, sensitivity, and humility (Global Digital Citizen Foundation, 2015b).

Global citizenship skills and processes, and the beneficial opportunities and possibilities that utilizing each creates, include the following.

- Recognizing and fostering global community:
  - Makes learners realize they are now part of a global culture and that time and distance barriers no longer exist
  - Creates awareness that technology connects learners with the world and its people instantaneously, and there are personal and communal responsibilities that come with this
  - Shows learners they have the means to help and support people all over the world rather than just in their smaller communities
  - Teaches learners more respect for the various traditions, values, faiths, beliefs, opinions, and practices of a global community
- Recognizing and fostering personal connections:
  - Helps learners see the benefits of being able to share their ideas with more people than ever before
  - Encourages acceptance, sensitivity, and humility in dealing with others
  - Teaches learners to see their marketplace as global, and recognize the significance of their ability to do business all over the world using shared technology
  - Helps learners understand that their peers and colleagues are all over the globe, and that many of these relationships must be virtually managed
  - Enables learners to foster and renew relationships with faraway people

# Digital Citizenship

Students who develop digital citizenship engage in appropriate and exemplary behavior online. This tenet helps develop a change in mindset, rather than simply regulating acceptable use policies, to affect safety in a transparent digital world. It shifts accountability for appropriate behavior to students, which fosters independence and personal responsibility (Global Digital Citizen Foundation, 2015b).

Digital citizenship skills and processes, and the beneficial opportunities and possibilities that utilizing each creates, include the following.

- Respect for self:
  - Increases awareness of portraying oneself positively online
  - Guides learners toward thinking critically about the short- and long-term effects of the information and images they post
  - Teaches learners the value of being private when necessary
  - Sets a positive example for others to follow
- Respect for others:
  - Encourages learning proper ways to communicate
  - Helps learners discover the consequences of behaviors such as bullying, flaming, harassing, and online stalking
  - Teaches learners the value of being constructive and friendly online
  - Helps learners respond to online conflicts with a sense of civility and constructive thinking
- Respect for property:
  - Teaches the importance of asking permission to share another's intellectual properties
  - Teaches how to cite sources and authorship properly to give credit to creators of intellectual property
  - Guides learners to explore fair use rules and copyright laws, and how they apply to sourcing and using online information
- Responsibility for self:
  - Helps learners avoid behavior that will put them at risk, both online and offline
  - Encourages exemplary personal governance as a habit of mind
  - Adds to learners' sense of self-worth and self-esteem
  - Reminds learners to safely and effectively password-protect information, property, and resources when appropriate
- Responsibility for others:
  - Encourages learners to discourage or report abusive and inappropriate behavior toward others

- Helps learners see the value in making others feel appreciated
- Discourages learners from forwarding or sharing potentially inappropriate or harmful information or images
- Responsibility for property:
  - Teaches learners the importance of treating their own property and others' with care and respect, including intellectual properties
  - Encourages learners to use free or open-source resources and to learn how to properly search for and recognize them
  - Reminds learners that any kind of digital piracy is still theft and that it is not a victimless crime
  - Teaches learners to act with integrity and to value what they use or own

# Altruistic Service

Altruistic service focuses on a healthy concern for others' well-being, including people we know as well as those we don't, and embraces opportunities to share charity and goodwill to benefit others. Altruistic service gives students opportunities to identify relevant and meaningful connections to the real world (Global Digital Citizen Foundation, 2015b).

Altruistic service skills and processes, and the beneficial opportunities and possibilities that utilizing each creates, include the following.

- Creating meaningful connections with others:
  - Helps learners begin to understand all the ways in which people are connected
  - Increases capacity for teaching and learning from others
  - Teaches the importance of having healthy relationships
  - Hones personal communication and interaction skills
- Practicing philanthropy and charity:
  - Fosters compassion and empathy, and helps learners grow personally
  - Helps learners realize that those less fortunate are not less deserving than they are
  - Helps learners act with civility and use proactive thinking toward others
  - Guides learners toward building a better space, community, and world environment
  - Teaches learners the value of sharing with others reasonably and fairly

- Establishing compassion by association:
  - Allows learners to serve others better by remembering how people helped them in the past
  - Teaches that many experiences are similar among all people, which lets us be more understanding and compassionate
  - Encourages constructively sharing mental and emotional burdens, making them lighter and more manageable

# Environmental Stewardship

Environmental stewardship demonstrates common sense values toward, and appreciation for, our natural environment. It encourages exploring how best to manage our use of Earth's resources—taking responsibility and action on personal, local, regional, national, and international levels (Global Digital Citizen Foundation, 2015b).

Environmental stewardship skills and processes, and the beneficial opportunities and possibilities that utilizing each creates, include the following.

- Managing resources:
  - Teaches learners to use resources wisely and to not be wasteful
  - Helps learners understand how people in poorer countries are able to live happily with much less
  - Looks toward a global community involvement in the economic usage of resources all people share
  - Contributes to the prosperity and longevity of future generations
- Caring for the environment:
  - Encourages learners to take pride in the places they call home—global, communal, and domestic
  - Directly affects personal health and wellness
  - Encourages habitually positive actions toward the environment that future generations can mirror
  - Reinforces the understanding that a healthy ecosystem is essential for all life to continue to prosper
- Responsibility for a global community:
  - Improves such economic industries as tourism, importing, and exporting
  - Brings cultures together for a mutually beneficial pursuit
  - Makes learners more mindful of conserving precious natural resources

- Helps learners discover just how necessary strong communities are for survival

# Global Digital Citizenship in Schools

Following are exemplars of inquiry- and project-based lessons that cultivate global digital citizenship. We've provided samples that cover a variety of grade levels and subjects to ensure all readers have access to relevant, applicable examples. Readers can find the full lessons as well as the activities and assessment resources on the Solution Fluency Activity Planner (https://solutionfluency.com). See the extensive rubrics at the end of this chapter (figures 8.1–8.5, pages 128–138) for tools to facilitate assessment of these and other global digital citizenship lessons.

## Schooled on the Future (Primary School)

**Essential question:** What do you think are three of the most significant changes that will affect the way schools and classrooms are run twenty years in the future?

**Subjects:** Social studies, language arts, history, technology

**Scenario:** Can you imagine what the classroom will look, sound, and feel like twenty years from now? What inventions will make their way into the students' hands? What new technologies and teacher training will your school need to invest in to transition to a new way of learning?

Your challenge is to create a time line showing the changes in schools (some of which should be at least a century ago) that have already happened and to continue the time line showing your predictions for twenty years ahead.

## Citizenship Day (Primary School)

Lessons that cultivate multiple fluencies appear in each applicable fluency.

**Essential question:** What can you do to help make people aware of online responsibility?

**Subjects:** Mathematics, technology, language arts, design

**Scenario:** Your group's task is to research all the practices of good digital citizenship, create unique class-participation games that teach people about digital citizenship, and invite other students and teachers (and even parents) to play and learn about digital citizenship during a class activity day.

Using what you learn, develop interactive games that teach people about how to practice good digital citizenship. Use the kinds of games you like to play or games you've seen on TV for ideas. Each group will create a unique game that is designed to teach the ideas of digital citizenship in a fun and creative way. Get your game on!

## Gratitude Group (Primary School)

Lessons that cultivate multiple fluencies appear in each applicable fluency.

**Essential question:** How could you use a public event to create awareness and express your appreciation for the people in your community?

**Subjects:** Language arts, social studies, mathematics

**Scenario:** Take a moment to think about the people who work to make the community strong through the services they provide to its economy. What would you come up with if you had one day to create a celebration to show these people how much you and your community appreciate them?

Create a unique community celebration showing appreciation for your community leaders and their day-to-day efforts. Use research about expressing thanks in cultures around the world, and make something to show your community how much it matters!

## Welcome, World! (Middle School)

**Essential question:** What common interests can students of different cultures share with each other using images and stories?

**Subjects:** Language arts, social studies, art, design

**Scenario:** Pictures can convey so many feelings and emotions, and you can also use them to share feelings about important points in your life or others' lives. Your school is going to incorporate a new student exchange program, and you've got a great idea. You're going to provide a promotional package for overseas students!

Create an online photo book to send to schools in different countries. Share details about what it's like to live and learn where you are from. With visuals and text, present your community and your school in a way that would help your reader to understand what makes your school and community unique or interesting. Capture exciting events or class projects and detail them in the photo book to turn it into an adventure!

## Radical Recyclers (Middle School)

**Essential question:** How can recycling help you with your own fundraising?

**Subjects:** Mathematics, economics, design, language arts

**Scenario:** Recycling events are a popular fundraising strategy for schools and other organizations. People donate recyclable items, from aluminum cans to computer components, and the money from recycling goes to the group that sponsored the recycling event.

A group of students at your school would like to organize a recycling fundraiser, but they need to convince your school principal that the project will be profitable. Use your mathematics skills to create scenarios for three different recyclable items, giving detailed calculations in the form of linear functions to make your case!

## Get What You Give (High School)

**Essential question:** How can we help people struggling in different regions of the world lead better lives?

**Subjects:** Economics, geography, civics, technology, design, language arts

**Scenario:** Students get to experience the spirit of giving while learning about the concept of microlending in this unit. They will get hands-on experience with how microlending sites work in order to give financial opportunities to struggling families on a global scale. At the same time, they will be learning about life in different parts of the world.

Form groups and visit Kiva (https://kiva.org), a leader in the microlending industry. Once you are familiar with how it works, you'll create a group account and begin looking for families you can help. Find out where in the world this person lives, and familiarize yourselves with the region and its physical and economical characteristics. Create a compelling two- to three-minute presentation, either digitally or traditionally, that is a profile of this individual and where he or she lives. Use both what you learned on Kiva and also the research you've done on where he or she lives. You must describe in detail why your group wants to sponsor him or her.

Next, what does your group want to do to raise money for your Kiva account? What about organizing a bake sale? How about designing and creating unique picture post-cards or calendars that you can sell? How about a bottle drive? Come up with an idea for your fundraiser, plan it out in detail, and put it into action to raise money. All the money you collect will go to helping the family you found on the Kiva website. You will be monitoring your account after you lend the money. When it's paid back, you can decide whether you wish to lend it again to a different person or withdraw it and donate it elsewhere.

## Biodiversity Database (High School)

**Essential question:** Using our knowledge of living organisms and their classification, how can we help solve environmental problems?

**Subjects:** Science, language arts, mathematics, technology, design

**Scenario:** For years, a freshwater pond in your community has been a popular fishing spot for area residents. Recently, however, the largemouth bass population in the pond has begun to deplete. The local conservation society has issued a request for proposals to solve the problem. You have decided to take on the challenge.

Create a biodiversity database to classify the various organisms that live in a fresh-water pond ecosystem. The database will be searchable on each organism's various characteristics. For example, if each organism is classified as a producer, consumer, or decomposer, you will be able to search the database to find all the producers, all the consumers, and all the decomposers. You will then use this information to explore the relationships between groups of living things in your community pond, with the goal of coming up with a creatively presented solution to the largemouth bass depletion problem.

# Rubrics for Global Digital Citizenship

We provide the following rubrics as examples for evaluating student performance on items that contribute to global digital citizenship, including descriptions of what student performance or work products might look like at each phase of the essential fluencies framework.

| Personal Responsibility | Phase 1 (awareness, connection, remembering) | Phase 2 (understanding, applying) | Phase 3 (analyzing, evaluating) | Phase 4 (evaluating, creating) |
|---|---|---|---|---|
| Integrity | • Sometimes acts with integrity in actions and words and occasionally considers others<br>• Possesses a sense of honesty and sometimes takes responsibility for his or her behavior or actions | • Often acts with integrity in actions and words<br>• Possesses a sense of honesty, justice, and fairness<br>• Usually considers others and interacts with dignity<br>• Will sometimes take responsibility for his or her behavior and actions and accepts the consequences | • Usually acts with integrity in actions and words<br>• Possesses a good sense of honesty, justice, and fairness<br>• Usually considers others and interacts with dignity<br>• Frequently takes responsibility for and reflects on his or her behavior and actions and the consequences | • Acts with integrity in actions and words<br>• Possesses a strong sense of honesty, justice, and fairness<br>• Considers others and interacts with dignity<br>• Takes responsibility for and reflects on his or her behavior, actions, and the consequences |

| Personal Responsibility | Phase 1 (awareness, connection, remembering) | Phase 2 (understanding, applying) | Phase 3 (analyzing, evaluating) | Phase 4 (evaluating, creating) |
|---|---|---|---|---|
| **Caring and compassion** | • Sometimes shows care and consideration to the people with whom he or she interacts<br>• Will sometimes offer support and show gratitude and appreciation | • Shows some care and consideration for others' needs<br>• Is sometimes supportive and will offer critique that is appropriate and suitable<br>• Often shows gratitude and appreciation | • Shows caring and consideration for others' needs and environment<br>• Is generally considerate in his or her actions and understands their impact<br>• Is generally suitably supportive and sometimes proactive<br>• Offers critique that is generally appropriate and suitable<br>• Shows gratitude and appreciation | • Shows caring and is empathetic to others' needs and the environment<br>• Is considerate and deliberate in his or her actions, weighing their impact before enacting them<br>• Is always supportive, proactive, and considerate<br>• Offers considerate critique that is appropriate and suitable<br>• Always shows genuine gratitude and appreciation |
| **Accountability** | • Shows awareness that his or her actions affect others and that others' actions affect him or her<br>• Will occasionally accept responsibility for his or her actions and attempt to change his or her behaviors | • Shows awareness that he or she has an impact on a personal and local scale<br>• Will consider his or her behaviors and actions, often taking responsibility, and will apply changes to behaviors and observe results | • Analyzes the impact of his or her behaviors and actions on a personal, local, and global scale<br>• Will frequently take responsibility and will often undertake measures to avoid, reduce, or minimize impacts | • Evaluates the impact of his or her behaviors and actions on a personal, local, and global scale<br>• Accepts responsibility and is proactive in undertaking what measures he or she can to avoid, reduce, or minimize impacts |
| **Curiosity** | • Sometimes demonstrates curiosity<br>• Occasionally shows enthusiasm for or a love of learning and discovery<br>• When encouraged, will develop skills that help him or her to focus and learn in his or her chosen or preferred areas | • Is often curious and inquiring<br>• Sometimes shows a love of learning and discovery, and shows potential to be a lifelong learner<br>• Will continue to develop skills that help focus on and learn new things in chosen or preferred areas | • Frequently is curious and inquiring<br>• Often shows a love of learning and discovery, enjoying opportunities to develop his or her understanding of the world<br>• Shows he or she is a lifelong learner who will often develop the skills and motivation required to continue his or her learning journey | • Is curious and inquiring, showing a love of learning and discovery, and actively seeking and enjoying opportunities to develop a deeper and richer understanding of the world<br>• Shows he or she is a lifelong learner who will develop and exhibit the skills and motivation required to continue his or her learning journey |

**Figure 8.1: Global digital citizen assessment rubric—Personal responsibility.**

continued →

| ♥ Personal Responsibility | Phase 1 (awareness, connection, remembering) | Phase 2 (understanding, applying) | Phase 3 (analyzing, evaluating) | Phase 4 (evaluating, creating) |
|---|---|---|---|---|
| Courage | • Will seldom challenge him- or herself, and can be impetuous and impulsive in his or her challenges and risk-taking<br>• Struggles to accept critique and criticism | • Is sometimes thoughtful and deliberate in his or her actions, but other times is impetuous<br>• May deliberately challenge him- or herself by undertaking tasks or participating in activities that are beyond his or her skill level or comfort zone, but prefers to remain within his or her comfort zone<br>• Can accept criticism with good grace and will sometimes reflect on it | • Is often thoughtful and deliberate in his or her actions<br>• Will sometimes deliberately challenge him- or herself, undertaking tasks or participating in activities that are beyond his or her skill level or comfort zone<br>• Will generally accept criticism with good grace and reflect on it | • Is always thoughtful and deliberate in his or her actions<br>• Will challenge him- or herself, undertaking tasks or participating in activities that are beyond his or her skill level or comfort zone, understanding that such endeavors will help him or her grow and develop<br>• Will accept criticism and reflect on it |
| Independence | • Shows little independence and requires extensive support to complete tasks | • Shows some independence and can complete most tasks with some support or guidance<br>• Shows ability to apply feedback to successfully complete tasks | • Shows ability to break the task into elements and then work through these with a degree of independence and self-management<br>• Requires little input or support and is often self-critical and can monitor his or her own progress<br>• Will often modify his or her planning and schedule as a result | • Shows ability to work effectively, efficiently, independently, or without close supervision or guidance<br>• Requires little or no input to successfully complete tasks<br>• Demonstrates ability to be self-critical and is able to monitor his or her own progress and reflect on it, and modifies his or her planning and schedule as a result |

| Personal Responsibility | Phase 1 (awareness, connection, remembering) | Phase 2 (understanding, applying) | Phase 3 (analyzing, evaluating) | Phase 4 (evaluating, creating) |
|---|---|---|---|---|
| Balance | • Has an awareness of his or her current state of balance, but struggles to take suitable steps to maintain a balanced lifestyle | • Attempts to be balanced in his or her physical, emotional, and intellectual well-being<br>• Will often apply changes to attempt to manage imbalances, though they are often reactive rather than proactive | • Often balanced in his or her physical, emotional, and intellectual health<br>• Can analyze his or her personal situation and take suitable steps to maintain or rebalance his or her needs and requirements<br>• Often considerate of the emotional, physical, and intellectual well-being of others | • Maintains constant balance in his or her physical, emotional, and intellectual health<br>• Can evaluate his or her personal situation and is often proactive in taking steps to maintain or rebalance his or her needs and requirements<br>• Considers his or her emotional, physical, and intellectual well-being and is considerate of others' requirements and needs in these aspects of life |
| Perseverance | • Occasionally shows determination<br>• Struggles to remain focused on tasks and goals, often quitting when the task becomes challenging | • Often shows a degree of determination and persistence<br>• Often remains focused on tasks and goals<br>• Sometimes moves beyond his or her comfort zone with encouragement to achieve a challenge or complete a task | • Often shows determination and persistence<br>• Shows ability to focus on achieving suitable challenges, goals, and objectives<br>• Can be reflective and refine his or her goals<br>• Is frequently realistic or optimistic, and will often move beyond his or her comfort zone to achieve a challenge or complete a task | • Shows constant determination and persistence, focusing on achieving suitable, considered challenges, goals, and objectives<br>• Always reflective and is able to, when required, refine goals and judge his or her progress toward milestones<br>• Demonstrates both realism and optimism<br>• Will readily move beyond his or her comfort zone to achieve a challenge or complete a task |

continued →

| Personal Responsibility | Phase 1 (awareness, connection, remembering) | Phase 2 (understanding, applying) | Phase 3 (analyzing, evaluating) | Phase 4 (evaluating, creating) |
|---|---|---|---|---|
| Resilience | • Struggles to accept criticism, often taking it as a personal slight<br>• When faced with a challenge, sometimes avoids it rather than persisting<br>• In a challenging situation, either completely avoids any form of support and assistance, or else relies completely on the support of others<br>• Struggles to maintain a mature outlook | • Will often accept criticism, sometimes applying suitable actions resulting from this<br>• Sometimes is persistent, occasionally overcoming adversity and intolerance<br>• Often seeks support when faced with challenges<br>• Shows a desire to work toward developing a mature, thoughtful, and determined outlook | • Shows progress toward developing resilience<br>• Shows ability to reflect on criticism, often taking on the relevant elements<br>• Frequently persists to overcome adversity and intolerance<br>• Faces challenges and often seeks support<br>• Frequently demonstrates a mature, thoughtful, and determined outlook on life | • Demonstrates constant resilience<br>• Shows ability to reflect on criticism, evaluating its worth and taking on the relevant elements<br>• Persists to overcome adversity and intolerance<br>• Faces both internal and external challenges realistically and seeks support when required<br>• Demonstrates a mature, thoughtful, and determined outlook on life |
| Efficiency | • Is sometimes accurate in his or her execution of the plan or product development | • Can apply the plan or design with some accuracy; there is some waste in terms of time, effort, and materials or resources | • Generally works efficiently, and there is minimal waste in terms of time, effort, and materials or resources<br>• Demonstrates general accuracy in the execution of his or her plan, product development, and his or her reflection | • Works with efficiency in a manner that is economical in terms of time, effort, and materials or resources<br>• Works with accuracy in the execution of his or her plans, product development, and reflection |
| Reflection | • Has some awareness of his or her strengths and weaknesses and can occasionally take actions to support him- or herself | • Is sometimes thoughtful and reflective<br>• Shows a broad understanding of his or her strengths and weaknesses and can sometimes take actions to support him- or herself or the community | • Is often thoughtful and reflective<br>• Analyzes his or her strengths and weaknesses and takes some thoughtful actions to support him- or herself, the community, and beyond | • Is constantly thoughtful and reflective<br>• Thoughtfully evaluates his or her actions, learning, and behaviors, and considers the strengths and weaknesses of these<br>• Takes actions to support him- or herself, the community, and beyond |

*Visit **go.SolutionTree.com/assessment** for a free reproducible version of this figure.*

| Global Citizenship | Phase 1 (awareness, connection, remembering) | Phase 2 (understanding, applying) | Phase 3 (analyzing, evaluating) | Phase 4 (evaluating, creating) |
|---|---|---|---|---|
| Global awareness | • Has an awareness of some of the broader global issues<br>• Is sometimes considerate and may report inappropriate behavior | • Displays characteristics of an emerging global citizen:<br>  • Shows some understanding of existing cultural, religious, and gender differences<br>  • Often shows respect for other peoples' customs and beliefs<br>  • Demonstrates that he or she is developing an understanding of the value and worth of diversity<br>  • Generally is intolerant of inappropriate behavior and occasionally takes steps to report it | • Displays characteristics of a developing global citizen:<br>  • Analyzes cultural, religious, and gender differences and uses them to guide his or her actions<br>  • Shows respect for other peoples' customs and beliefs<br>  • Will sometimes value and celebrate differences as part of a rich human tapestry<br>  • Generally is intolerant of racist, abusive, sexist, or inappropriate behavior and sometimes takes steps to report it | • Displays the characteristics of a global citizen:<br>  • Considers and evaluates cultural, religious, and gender differences and mediates his or her actions and interactions by considering them<br>  • Consistently shows respect and care for other peoples' customs and beliefs<br>  • Values and celebrates differences as part of a rich human tapestry<br>  • Shows intolerance of racist, abusive, sexist, or inappropriate behavior and takes, where possible, the appropriate steps to prevent or report it |
| Political awareness | • Has little understanding of governance or current issues<br>• Will often be guided to support a particular stance, party, or standpoint | • Has an understanding of the governance from a local, national, and global perspective<br>• Has some depth of understanding of some historical, current, and emerging issues<br>• Follows the legal requirements for participation in local and national events | • Shows a developing sense of political awareness<br>• Has an understanding of governance from a local, national, and global perspective<br>• Analyzes historical, current, and emerging issues and breaks them down into their components<br>• Can provide some limited evaluation of bias<br>• Forms his or her own political stance on issues and may support parties, groups, or organizations that support his or her viewpoint | • Shows political awareness and is a contributing member of society<br>• Has a broad understanding of governance from a local, national, and global perspective<br>• Analyzes and evaluates historical, current, and emerging issues, separating the issue from political rhetoric, bias, and media spin<br>• Forms his or her own political stance on issues that are critical to him or her and supports parties, groups, or organizations that uphold an appropriate ethical and moral standpoint |

*Visit* **go.SolutionTree.com/assessment** *for a free reproducible version of this figure.*

**Figure 8.2: Global digital citizen assessment rubric—Global citizenship.**

| Digital Citizenship | Phase 1 (awareness, connection, remembering) | Phase 2 (understanding, applying) | Phase 3 (analyzing, evaluating) | Phase 4 (evaluating, creating) |
|---|---|---|---|---|
| **Respect and responsibility for oneself** | • Has an awareness of some of the online risks and appropriate strategies for personal online safety<br><br>• Sometimes takes steps to protect him- or herself | • Frequently applies appropriate strategies in his or her online behavior and to minimize exposure to risk<br><br>• Takes some steps to protect his or her integrity, privacy, data, or identity<br><br>• Sometimes seeks support or reports abuse | • Will often be considerate with his or her online behavior<br><br>• Takes steps to protect his or her integrity, privacy, data, and identity<br><br>• Analyzes and evaluates his or her situation and takes steps to minimize his or her exposure to risk<br><br>• Often seeks support and reports abuse to relevant authorities | • Shows regular deliberation and consideration of his or her online behavior<br><br>• Takes suitable steps to protect his or her integrity, privacy, data, and identity<br><br>• Evaluates his or her situation and is both proactive and reactive toward minimizing his or her exposure to risk<br><br>• Seeks support and reports abuse to relevant authorities |
| **Respect and responsibility for others** | • Has an awareness of the guidelines, norms, and protocols for interactions with other people in a digital environment<br><br>• Can sometimes be respectful and considerate in his or her interactions | • Follows the guidelines, norms, and protocols for interactions with other people in a digital environment<br><br>• Is generally respectful and considerate in his or her interactions | • Is often considerate in his or her online behavior<br><br>• Often considers others' needs and privacy<br><br>• Is predominantly respectful in his or her interactions and considerate of other cultures and perspectives<br><br>• Often shows intolerance for abuse<br><br>• Considers situations and often takes steps to protect the safety and security of others | • Shows consistent deliberation and consideration in his or her online behavior<br><br>• Considers others' needs and privacy<br><br>• Is respectful in his or her interactions, considerate of other cultures and perspectives, and intolerant of abuse<br><br>• Evaluates and considers situations on an ethical and moral basis and will take appropriate steps to protect the safety, privacy, security, and identity of others |

| Digital Citizenship | Phase 1 (awareness, connection, remembering) | Phase 2 (understanding, applying) | Phase 3 (analyzing, evaluating) | Phase 4 (evaluating, creating) |
|---|---|---|---|---|
| **Respect and responsibility for property** | • Has an awareness of the laws of copyright, intellectual property, and privacy<br><br>• Occasionally cites sources in a suitable manner | • Can follow the guidelines and norms for digital property<br><br>• Shows an understanding of the laws surrounding copyright, intellectual property, and privacy and sometimes applies them<br><br>• Occasionally requests permission to use resources and suitably cites sources | • Is often thoughtful in his or her online actions<br><br>• Shows a general understanding of the laws surrounding copyright, intellectual property, and privacy and often applies them<br><br>• Sometimes requests permission to use property and acknowledges ownership and cites resources | • Shows consistent deliberation and consideration in his or her online actions<br><br>• Possesses a deep and rich understanding of the laws surrounding copyright, intellectual property, and privacy and is able to apply them ethically<br><br>• Requests permission to use property and abides by the owners' rights to deny use<br><br>• Is always respectful and responsible in acknowledging ownership and citing resources and in protecting and securing sites and data<br><br>• Is considerate of and reciprocal to others' requests to use his or her intellectual property |

*Visit **go.SolutionTree.com/assessment** for a free reproducible version of this figure.*

**Figure 8.3: Global digital citizen assessment rubric—Digital citizenship.**

| ![dove] Altruistic Service | Phase 1 (awareness, connection, remembering) | Phase 2 (understanding, applying) | Phase 3 (analyzing, evaluating) | Phase 4 (evaluating, creating) |
|---|---|---|---|---|
| Problem finding | • Struggles to identify problems independently and frequently requires support and guidance | • Describes and explains situations or issues on a local, regional, or global scale<br>• Can broadly consider the level of need and some potential impacts that his or her support could make | • Analyzes situations or issues on a local, regional, or global scale and breaks them down into their components<br>• Can identify and consider areas of need, the level of need, and some potential impacts that his or her support could make<br>• Investigates and researches the concern | • Analyzes and evaluates situations or issues on a local, regional, or global scale to identify areas of need<br>• Considers and evaluates the level of need and the impact that his or her support can make in resolving this<br>• Investigates and researches the concern to discern if the need is genuine, legitimate, and worthy of support |
| Problem solving | • Is often involved in service superficially, minimally, or as a matter of compliance to school or organizational requirements | • Understands the need for altruistic service, and actively participates in service<br>• Often reviews his or her actions | • Analyzes the need for altruistic service<br>• Provides limited or superficial evaluation of the need<br>• Develops and structures a plan or process that will partly help to resolve the issue or need<br>• Actively undertakes altruistic service, including supporting and organizing, and reviews his or her actions | • Evaluates the need for altruistic service and validates that need, ensuring that his or her actions or support will be beneficial to the intended recipient<br>• Develops and structures a plan or process that helps resolve or mitigate the issue or need<br>• Arranges, organizes, promotes, supports, or enacts altruistic service in its varied forms through action or service<br>• Actively reviews and critiques his or her process and refines, adjusts, or terminates his or her actions as required |

*Visit* **go.SolutionTree.com/assessment** *for a free reproducible version of this figure.*

**Figure 8.4: Global digital citizen assessment rubric—Altruistic service.**

| Environmental Stewardship | Phase 1 (awareness, connection, remembering) | Phase 2 (understanding, applying) | Phase 3 (analyzing, evaluating) | Phase 4 (evaluating, creating) |
|---|---|---|---|---|
| **Personal awareness and action** | • Has some awareness of environmental issues that impact him or her<br><br>• Sometimes participates in actions to reduce environmental impact or damage | • Often shows interest in his or her environment<br><br>• Has some understanding of the impact of his or her actions and those of the community and nation on the environment<br><br>• Sometimes takes personal responsibility for his or her actions and undertakes actions to reduce the environmental cost | • Shows interest in his or her environment<br><br>• Can analyze short- and long-term impacts of his or her actions and those of the community and nation on the environment and break them down into their components<br><br>• Often takes personal responsibility for his or her actions and undertakes suitable and sustainable actions to reduce the environmental cost | • Shows an active interest in his or her environment, analyzing and evaluating the short- and long-term impact of his or her actions and lifestyle and those of the community and nation on the environment<br><br>• Takes personal responsibility for his or her actions and moderates his or her behaviors and actions to reduce the environmental cost<br><br>• Investigates, evaluates, and undertakes whatever preventative, restorative, and sustainable measures are feasible |
| **Global awareness and action** | • Has an awareness of some of the environmental issues and, when encouraged, may participate in activities to reduce or raise awareness of them | • Has an interest in and understanding of some environmental issues<br><br>• Supports local environmental activities, sometimes taking a stand on significant issues | • Shows an interest in global environmental issues and will investigate causes or concerns before offering support<br><br>• Often takes a stand on current matters, undertaking appropriate actions that raise awareness<br><br>• Sometimes shows stewardship of his or her world | • Shows an active interest in global environmental issues<br><br>• Validates causes or concerns before offering support<br><br>• Takes a stand on matters of importance, undertaking appropriate actions that raise awareness of concerns through legitimate and appropriate means<br><br>• Shows stewardship, care, and responsibility for his or her world<br><br>• Thinks globally while acting locally |

**Figure 8.5: Global digital citizen assessment rubric—Environmental stewardship.**

continued →

| Environmental Stewardship | Phase 1 (awareness, connection, remembering) | Phase 2 (understanding, applying) | Phase 3 (analyzing, evaluating) | Phase 4 (evaluating, creating) |
|---|---|---|---|---|
| Environmental stewardship as a consumer | • Has awareness of environmental issues associated with the production, distribution, and disposal of products<br>• Can sometimes consider these factors when making a purchase | • Understands the importance of purchasing power<br>• Understands some of the environmental or societal costs of purchases, supply chains, and manufacturing processes<br>• Is often guided by product labeling as a form of ethical or moral guidance<br>• Applies general guidelines for appropriate purchases | • Understands the impact of purchasing power as a force for change<br>• Analyzes the environmental or societal cost of his or her purchases, the supply chain, and manufacturing base<br>• Analyzes product labeling and often makes informed decisions regarding purchases based on his or her overall analysis<br>• Makes purchasing decisions that may be influenced by ethical and moral issues | • Considers the impact of purchasing power as a force for change<br>• Evaluates the environmental and societal cost of his or her purchases, the supply chain, and manufacturing base before making a decision to buy<br>• Analyzes and evaluates product labeling and makes informed decisions regarding purchases<br>• Makes purchasing decisions based on an informed ethical and moral stance |

Visit **go.SolutionTree.com/assessment** for a free reproducible version of this figure.

Our simple wish for the bright future is to see all beings reflect and grow as global digital citizens. We imagine a world where we all evaluate our thoughts and actions, and we like it. To challenge our youth with the attributes listed in this framework is a great place to start.

# Guiding Questions

Answer the following questions as an individual or with your school team.

1. In your own words, how would you describe what being a global digital citizen both entails and represents?

2. How has our level of interconnectedness heightened our responsibilities for ourselves and each other as global citizens?

3. What are the advantages and disadvantages of living so much of our lives in online environments?

4. What skills and mindsets from all the other fluencies are reflected in global digital citizenship?

5. How can global digital citizenship practices preserve and improve our quality of life for future generations?

## *Epilogue*
# Where Will You Go From Here?

In this book, we've given you a glimpse of six essential fluencies to apply to innovative learning practices. We've discussed the skills and mindsets that each one fosters, and the inherent benefits of each. Finally, we've given you a framework for assessing their application and practices in any classroom setting you may be working in. That said, these fluencies do not only apply to life inside school. As you begin working with the fluencies, realize you are not merely giving your students skills for school. You're giving them skills for life.

The fluencies can be applied to every facet of modern life. We've designed them to be simple, practical, and highly learnable. Many educators see them for the first time and fear they may be too complicated or involved to take on, but the truth is that they are meant to eventually become a natural part of all aspects of our lives.

Solution fluency is applicable to everything from solving a global crisis to making a grocery list. We use information fluency for simple searches and complex research projects. Our creativity fluency shines whether we doodle an idea on a sketch pad or design something that changes the world forever. We are employing unconscious media fluency skills whenever we watch a video, look at an advertisement, view a presentation, or create any of these items ourselves. Our teamwork successes and leadership capabilities come to the forefront as we use collaboration fluency. And we look to the future, and to our students' future, as we consider how they will go into the world and transform it with the mindset of the global digital citizen.

These are the gifts we can impart to our students now, using the fluencies in our modern teaching and learning practices. We can't wait for others to do it, because change starts with us. This is how we create problem solvers, independent thinkers, and lifelong learners. Acting in the present is how we build the future. Beautiful and powerful change happens one step at a time and one student at a time. The key to true transformation and growth is stepping outside the norm and doing something you've never done before.

We see a bright future for all beings created by a caring, compassionate, solutions-focused generation, striving together, transcending borders, and overcoming challenges to solve real-world problems that matter as responsible, ethical global digital citizens.

What do you see? Where do you want to go, and where will you begin?

# Glossary of Command Terms

*Source: Adapted from Command Terms, n.d.; International Baccalaureate Organization, 2011a, 2011b; Quizlet, 2015; smannino7, 2011; TagMath, n.d.*

Reaching a consensus is often difficult. Clearly defined command terms will help teachers have a common understanding of what success at each phase looks like. The following terms are a solid start.

**analyze.** Break down to bring out the essential elements or structure.

**annotate.** Add brief notes to a diagram or graph.

**calculate.** Obtain a numerical answer showing the relevant stages in the working.

**classify.** Arrange or order by class or category.

**compare.** Give an account of the similarities between two (or more) items or scenarios, referring to both (all) of them throughout.

**construct.** Display information in a diagrammatic or logical form.

**contrast.** Give an account of the differences between two (or more) items or situations, referring to both (all) of them throughout.

**define.** Give the precise meaning of a word, phrase, concept, or physical quantity.

**demonstrate.** Prove or make clear by reasoning or evidence, illustrating and explaining with examples or practical application.

**describe.** Give a detailed account.

**determine.** Obtain the answers, showing all relevant work. *Find* and *calculate* can also be used.

**differentiate.** Obtain the derivative of a function.

**discuss.** Offer a thoughtful and balanced review that includes a range of arguments, factors, or hypotheses. Opinions or conclusions should be presented clearly and supported by appropriate evidence.

**distinguish.** Make clear the differences between two or more concepts or items.

**draw.** Represent by means of a labeled, accurate diagram or graph. Diagrams should be drawn to scale. Graphs should have points correctly plotted (if appropriate) and joined in a straight line or smooth curve.

**estimate.** Obtain an approximate value.

**evaluate.** Make an appraisal by weighing the strengths and limitations.

**explain.** Give a detailed account, including reasons or causes.

**find.** Obtain the answers showing all relevant work. *Calculate* and *determine* can also be used.

**formulate.** Express precisely and systematically the relevant concepts or arguments.

**identify.** Provide an answer from a number of possibilities.

**integrate.** Obtain the integral of a function.

**justify.** Give valid reasons or evidence to support an answer or conclusion.

**label.** Add identifiers to a diagram.

**outline.** Give a brief account or summary.

**solve.** Obtain the solutions or roots of an equation.

**state.** Give a specific name, value, or other brief answer without explanation or calculation.

**suggest.** Propose a solution, hypothesis, or other possible answer.

**to what extent.** Consider the merits or otherwise of an argument or concept. Opinions and conclusions should be presented clearly and supported with appropriate evidence and sound arguments.

# References and Resources

Anderson, L. W., & Krathwohl, D. (Eds.). (2001). *A taxonomy for learning, teaching, and assessing: A revision of Bloom's taxonomy of educational objectives.* New York: Longman.

Applebaum, B. (2015, May 17). Perils of globalization when factories close and towns struggle. *New York Times.* Accessed at www.nytimes.com/2015/05/18 /business/a-decade-later-loss-of-maytag-factory-still-resonates.html on May 16, 2016.

Ausubel, D. P., Novak, J. D., & Hanesian, H. (1978). *Educational psychology: A cognitive view* (2nd ed.). New York: Holt, Rinehart and Winston.

Big Picture Education Australia. (2011). *The big commitment: What we expect of Big Picture students.* Accessed at http://yulebrookcollege.wa.edu.au/component /phocadownload/category/5-about-yule-brook-college.html?download=7 :what-we-expect-from-big-picture-students on May 5, 2016.

Black, P., Harrison, C., Lee, C., Marshall, B., & Wiliam, D. (2003). *Assessment for learning: Putting it into practice.* Maidenhead, England: Open University Press.

Black, P., & Wiliam, D. (1998). Assessment and classroom learning. *Assessment in Education: Principles, Policy and Practice, 5*(1), 7–74.

Bloom, B. S. (Ed.). (1956). *Taxonomy of educational objectives: Handbook I— Cognitive domain.* White Plains, NY: Longman.

Broadfoot, P., Daugherty, R., Gardner, J., Harlen, W., James, M., & Stobart, G. (2002). *Assessment for learning: 10 principles—Research-based principles to guide classroom practice.* Accessed at http://methodenpool.uni-koeln.de /benotung/assessment_basis.pdf on August 12, 2015.

Churches, A. (n.d.). *A guide to formative and summative assessment and rubric development.* Accessed at http://aadmc.wikispaces.com/file/view/Assessment .pdf on August 13, 2015.

Churches, A. (2008, September 9). *21st century assessment.* Accessed at http:// edorigami.wikispaces.com/21st+Century+Assessment on February 2, 2016.

Churches, A. (2009, March 31). *Bloom's digital taxonomy.* Accessed at http:// edorigami.wikispaces.com/file/view/bloom's+Digital+taxonomy+v3.01.pdf on February 2, 2016.

*Command terms.* (n.d.). Accessed at https://hhs.canyonsdistrict.org/docs/IB /Command_Terms_2016.pdf on July 28, 2016.

Crockett, L., Jukes, I., & Churches, A. (2011). *Literacy is not enough: 21st-century fluencies for the digital age.* Thousand Oaks, CA: Corwin Press.

Dinh, L. (2015). Unity week. *Life in the Wilderness, 5,* 2.

Dinham, S. (2008a, May). Feedback on feedback. *Teacher: The National Education Magazine,* 20–23.

Dinham, S. (2008b). Powerful teacher feedback. *Synergy, 6*(2), 35–38.

Friedman, T. L. (2005). *The world is flat: A brief history of the twenty-first century.* New York: Farrar, Strauss & Giroux.

Gardner, J., Harlen, W., Hayward, L., & Stobart, G. (2008). *Changing assessment practice: Process, principles and standards.* Accessed at www .nuffieldfoundation.org/sites/default/files/JG%20Changing%20 Assment%20Practice%20Final%20Final(1).pdf on August 12, 2015.

Global Digital Citizen Foundation. (2015a, June 11). *Bloom's digital taxonomy verbs* [Infographic]. Accessed at http://globaldigitalcitizen.org/blooms-digital -taxonomy-verbs-infographic on October 30, 2015.

Global Digital Citizen Foundation. (2015b). *Global digital citizen.* Accessed at http://globaldigitalcitizen.org/21st-century-fluencies/global-digital -citizenship on August 13, 2015.

Gronlund, N. E. (1998). *Assessment of student achievement* (6th ed.). Boston: Allyn & Bacon.

Hattie, J. (2009). *Visible learning: A synthesis of over 800 meta-analyses relating to achievement.* London: Routledge.

Hattie, J. (2012). *Visible learning for teachers: Maximizing impact on learning.* New York: Routledge.

Hattie, J., & Timperley, H. (2007). The power of feedback. *Review of Educational Research, 77*(1), 81–112.

Holmes-Smith, P. (2005). *Assessment* for *learning: Using statewide literacy and numeracy tests as diagnostic tools.* Accessed at http://research.acer.edu.au /cgi/viewcontent.cgi?article=1009&context=research_conference_2005 on August 12, 2015.

IBM. (n.d.). *Bringing big data to the enterprise.* Accessed at https://www-01.ibm.com /software/data/bigdata/what-is-big-data.html on July 11, 2016.

International Baccalaureate Organization. (2011a). *IBDP environmental systems and societies student handbook: 2010–2011.* Accessed at http://integration21.ru /foreing/ES&S%20HANDBOOK.pdf on August 13, 2015.

International Baccalaureate Organization. (2011b). *Geography guide: First examinations 2011.* Accessed at http://phsibsupport.org/wp-content/uploads /2013/11/IB-Geography-Guide.pdf on August 13, 2015.

Janz, W. (2011). This is Flint, Michigan, in all its pain and all its glory. *Grist.* Accessed at http://grist.org/urbanism/2011-02-15-this-is-flint-michigan on May 16, 2016.

Klingberg, T. (2009). *The overflowing brain: Information overload and the limits of working memory.* New York: Oxford University Press.

The Learning Management Corporation. (n.d.). *Writing effective questions.* Accessed at www.thelearningmanager.com/pubdownloads/writing_effective _questions.pdf on August 12, 2015.

Lee, M. A., & Mather, M. (2008). U.S. labor force trends. *Popular Bulletin, 63*(2), 1–20. Accessed at www.prb.org/pdf08/63.2uslabor.pdf on May 16, 2016.

Marker, S. (2015, February 22). *How many jobs will the average person have in his or her lifetime?* [Blog post]. Accessed at www.linkedin.com/pulse/how-many -jobs-average-person-have-his-her-lifetime-scott-marker on May 16, 2016.

Masters, G. N. (2013). *Reforming educational assessment: Imperatives, principles and challenges.* Camberwell, Victoria: Australian Council for Educational Research. Accessed at http://research.acer.edu.au/cgi/viewcontent.cgi?article =1021&context=aer on August 12, 2015.

Medina, J. (2008). *Brain rules: 12 principles for surviving and thriving at work, home, and school.* Seattle, WA: Pear Press.

National Governors Association Center for Best Practices & Council of Chief State School Officers. (2010a). *Common Core State Standards for English language arts and literacy in history/social studies, science, and technical subjects.* Washington, DC: Authors. Accessed at www.corestandards.org/assets/CCSSI _ELA%20Standards.pdf on August 13, 2015.

National Governors Association Center for Best Practices & Council of Chief State School Officers. (2010b). *Common Core State Standards for mathematics.* Washington, DC: Authors. Accessed at www.corestandards.org/assets /CCSSI_Math%20Standards.pdf on August 13, 2015.

New South Wales Department of Education and Training. (2008a). *Effective feedback and E assessment: School based assessment and reporting unit curriculum K–12 directorate* [PowerPoint presentation]. Accessed at www.curriculumsupport .education.nsw.gov.au/digital_rev/assessment/assets/docs/efffective _feedbackv2.ppt on August 12, 2015.

New South Wales Department of Education and Training. (2008b, August). *Principles of assessment and reporting in NSW Public Schools.* Accessed at www.curriculumsupport.education.nsw.gov.au/timetoteach/policy_doc /principles_ar.pdf on August 12, 2015.

Nyquist, J. (2003). *The benefits of reconstructing feedback as a larger system of formative assessment: A meta-analysis.* Unpublished master's thesis, Vanderbilt University, Nashville, TN.

Padnani, A. (2013, December 8). Anatomy of Detroit's decline. *New York Times.* Accessed at www .nytimes.com/interactive/2013/08/17/us/detroit-decline.html?_r=0 on May 16, 2016.

Pink, D. H. (2005). *A whole new mind: Moving from the information age to the conceptual age.* New York: Riverhead Books.

Pink, D. H. (2011). *Drive: The surprising truth about what motivates us.* New York: Riverhead Books.

Quizlet. (2015). *IB geography vocabulary: Urban environments.* Accessed at https:// quizlet.com/43797350/ib-geography-vocabulary-urban-environments-flash -cards on August 13, 2015.

smannino7. (2011, June). *IB economics command terms.* Accessed at www.cram.com /flashcards/ib-economics-command-terms-1807386 on August 13, 2015.

Stevenson, M. (2007). *Education 3.0 presentation notes.* Accessed at http://tools.cisco .com/cmn/jsp/index.jsp?id=73088&redir=YES&userid=(none) on February 2, 2016.

TagMath. (n.d.). *Command terms.* Accessed at http://tagmath.org/math/command -terms on August 13, 2015.

Te Kete Ipurangi. (n.d.). *Principles of assessment for learning.* Accessed at http:// assessment.tki.org.nz/Assessment-in-the-classroom/Underlying-principles -of-assessment-for-learning/Principles-of-assessment-for-learning on February 2, 2016.

Wiggins, G. (1990). The case for authentic assessment. *Eric Digest.* Accessed at http://files.eric.ed.gov/fulltext/ED328611.pdf on May 16, 2016.

Wiggins, G., & McTighe, J. (2005). *Understanding by design* (Expanded 2nd ed.). Alexandria, VA: Association for Supervision and Curriculum Development.

Wiliam, D. (2011). *Embedded formative assessment.* Bloomington, IN: Solution Tree Press.

Wyse, D., Hayward, L., & Pandya, J. (2015). *The SAGE handbook of curriculum, pedagogy and assessment.* Thousand Oaks, CA: SAGE.

Yip, J. (2016, February 21). *It's not just standing up: Patterns for daily standup meetings.* Accessed at http://martinfowler.com/articles/itsNotJustStandingUp .html on July 27, 2016.

Zehr, H. (1990). *Changing lenses: A new focus for crime and justice.* Scottdale, PA: Herald Press.

# Index

## A

acquire stage, 59–60, 68–69
altruistic service, 123–124, 136
analyze stage, 60–63, 70
Anderson, L. W., 10, 30
apply stage, 63–64, 71–72
ask stage, 57–59, 67
"Assessment and Classroom Learning" (Black and Wiliam), 18
assessment
　　*as* learning, 11, 12
　　common language, need for, 2, 9–31
　　*for* learning, 11, 12
　　future of, 5–7
　　need to change, 4–5
　　*of* learning, 11, 12
　　summative, 2–3
　　types of, 12
assess stage, 64–65, 72
Australian Curriculum, 44
Ausubel, D. P., 14

## B

Big Picture Education Australia, 5–6
Black, P., 12, 18
blogging sites, 23

## B

Bloom, B. S., 10, 18, 26
Bloom's taxonomy, 10, 26–28
　　digital taxonomy verbs, 30–31
*Brain Rules* (Medina), 89

## C

Churches, A., xvi, 3, 37
collaboration fluency
　　defined, xvii
　　engineer stage, 106, 115
　　envision stage, 105, 113–114
　　establish stage, 103–104, 111–112
　　examine stage, 107–108, 117
　　execute stage, 106–107, 116
　　implementing, in schools, 108–111
　　rubrics, 111–117
command terms, 29, 31, 32, 33, 143–144
Council of Chief State School Officers (CCSSO), 3, 37
creativity fluency
　　defined, xvii
　　identify stage, 75–76, 83
　　image stage, 79, 86
　　implementing, in schools, 80–83
　　inspect stage, 79–80, 87
　　inspire stage, 77–78, 84
　　interpolate stage, 78–79, 85

rubrics, 83–87

criterion-based assessment tools, 28–36

Crockett, L., xvi, 37

D

debrief strategies, 43, 54

define strategies, 37–38, 47

deliver strategies, 42–43, 53

design strategies, 40–42, 51–52

diagnostic assessment
        forms of, 15–18
        outcomes, 13
        role of, 10–11, 12–15

digital citizenship, 121–123, 133–134

Dinham, S., 19–20

discover strategies, 38–39, 48–49

domains of learning, 26

dream strategies, 39–40, 50

E

*Educational Psychology: A Cognitive View* (Ausubel), 14

engineer stage, 106, 115

environmental stewardship, 124–125, 137–138

envision stage, 105, 113–114

establish stage, 103–104, 111–112

evidence statements, 31–32, 33

examine stage, 107–108, 117

execute stage, 106–107, 116

F

feedback
        high-quality, 20–24
        importance of, 9
        Model of Effective Feedback, 21–23

5As, xvii, 57–65, 67–72

5Es, xvii, 103–117

5Is, xvii, 75–87

fluencies
        defined, xvii–xviii

description of essential, xvi–xvii, 25

fluencies assessment framework
        common assessment language, need for, 29–31
        criterion-based assessment tools, 28–36
        evidence statements, 31–32, 33
        exemplars of student work, 32–34
        phases of, 26–28
        quantity modifications, 34–36

formative assessment
        defined, 18
        high-quality feedback, 20–24
        role of, 11, 12, 18–20

G

global citizenship, 121, 135

global digital citizenship
        altruistic service, 123–124, 136
        defined, xvii, 119
        digital citizenship, 121–123, 133–134
        environmental stewardship, 124–125, 137–138
        global citizenship, 121, 135
        implementing, in schools, 125–128
        personal responsibility, 119–120, 128–132
        rubrics, 128–138

H

Harrison, C., 12

Hattie, J., 9, 19, 20, 21

Hayward, L., 14

higher-order thinking skills (HOTS), 10, 26

I

iBooks, 23

identify stage, 75–76, 83

image stage, 79, 86

information fluency
        acquire stage, 59–60, 68–69

analyze stage, 60–63, 70
  apply stage, 63–64, 71–72
  ask stage, 57–59, 67
  assess stage, 64–65, 72
  defined, xvi–xvii
  implementing, in schools, 65–67
  rubrics, 67–72
inspect stage, 79–80, 87
inspire stage, 77–78, 84
International Baccalaureate Organization (IBO), 28
interpolate stage, 78–79, 85

J
Jukes, I., xvi, 37

K
Klingberg, T., 37
knowledge acquisition, 10, 11
knowledge creation, 10, 11
knowledge deepening, 10, 11
knowledge of correct results (KCR), 22, 23
knowledge of correct results and explanation (KCR+e), 22, 23
knowledge of results (KoR), 21–22, 23
Krathwohl, D., 10, 30

L
lean methodology, 4–5
learning domains. See domains of learning
Learning Management Corporation, 16
learning process, 10–12
Lee, C., 12
leverage, 91–93, 99–102
listen, 89–91, 96–98
Literacy Is Not Enough (Crockett, Jukes, and Churches), xvi, 37
lower-order thinking skills (LOTS), 10, 26

M
Mahara, 24
Marshall, B., 12

McTighe, J., 14
media fluency
  defined, xvii
  implementing, in schools, 93–95
  leverage, 91–93, 99–102
  listen, 89–91, 96–98
  rubrics, 95–102
Medina, J., 89
Melrose High School, 6
Microsoft Word, 4
Model of Effective Feedback, 21–23

N
National Governors Association Center for Best Practices, (NGA), 3, 37
New South Wales (NSW) Department of Education and Training, 18–19
New Zealand Curriculum framework, 28
Nyquist, J., 9, 10, 21–23

O
Overflowing Brain, The (Klingberg), 37

P
Pandya, J., 14
personal responsibility, 119–120, 128–132
Pink, D. H., 25
portfolios, 22–23
Principles of Assessment and Reporting in NSW Public Schools, 18–19
prosumers, 4

Q
questions, guidelines for writing effective multiple-choice, 16–17

R
rubrics
  collaboration fluency, 111–117
  command term definitions, 31
  creativity fluency, 83–87
  evidence statements, 31–32, 33

example of basic, 29
global digital citizenship, 128–138
information fluency, 67–72
media fluency, 95–102
quantity modifications, 34–36
solution fluency, 46–54

## S

6Ds, xvi, 37–43, 46–54
skills, description of essential, xvi
SMOG, 15
solution fluency
    debrief strategies, 43, 54
    defined, xvi
    define strategies, 37–38, 47
    deliver strategies, 42–43, 53
    design strategies, 40–42, 51–52
    discover strategies, 38–39, 48–49
    dream strategies, 39–40, 50
    implementing, in schools, 44–46
    rubrics, 46–54
Stevenson, M., 10

summative assessments, 2–3, 11–12

## T

terminology, need for common assessment, 29–31
Tertiary Education Commission, 24
3As, 25
Timperley, H., 20
2Ls, xvii, 89–102

## U

*Understanding by Design* (Wiggins and McTighe), 14

*Visible Learning* (Hattie), 9

## W

Wiggins, G., 14
Wilderness School, 23, 44
Wiliam, D., 12, 18
WordPress, 23
Wyse, D., 14

### The Myth of the Muse
*Douglas Reeves and Brooks Reeves*
The authors argue that creativity is not spontaneous or inborn but a process that can be cultivated. Ideal for team study and discussion, the book outlines seven virtues that inspire creativity and includes activities and guidelines to encourage and facilitate creativity.
**BKF655**

### Deeper Learning
*Edited by James A. Bellanca*
Education authorities from around the globe draw on research as well as their own experience to explore deeper learning, a process that promotes higher-order thinking, reasoning, and problem solving to better educate students and prepare them for college and careers.
**BKF622**

### Solutions for Modern Learning Series
This thought-provoking collection engages educators in a powerful conversation about learning and schooling in the connected world. Each title challenges traditional thinking about education and helps to develop the modern contexts teachers and leaders need to effectively support digital learners.
**BKF687, BKF692, BKF688, BKF693, BKF686, BKF685**

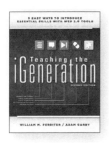

### Teaching the iGeneration
*William M. Ferriter and Adam Garry*
Find the natural overlap between the work you already believe in and the digital tools that define today's learning. Each chapter introduces an enduring life skill and a digital solution to enhance traditional skill-based instructional practices. A collection of handouts and supporting materials ends each chapter.
**BKF671**

**Solution Tree | Press** a division of
Solution Tree

Visit SolutionTree.com or call 800.733.6786 to order.

# "Excellent engagement
in what truly matters
in **assessment**.

# Great examples!"